Hans Friedrich Gadow

A Classification of Vertebrata, Recent and Extinct

Hans Friedrich Gadow

A Classification of Vertebrata, Recent and Extinct

ISBN/EAN: 9783337179250

Printed in Europe, USA, Canada, Australia, Japan

Cover: Foto ©Thomas Meinert / pixelio.de

More available books at **www.hansebooks.com**

A CLASSIFICATION OF VERTEBRATA

RECENT AND EXTINCT

BY

HANS GADOW, M.A., Ph.D., F.R.S.

CAMBRIDGE

LONDON
ADAM AND CHARLES BLACK
1898

INTRODUCTORY

The diagnoses given in this classification are not exhaustive definitions, although often more than sufficient because of what may be called additional characters. For instance, the "possession of visceral arches, one pair of which is modified into jaws," is a quite sufficient diagnosis of the Gnathostomata. The presence of an anterior and a posterior pair of limbs is probably quite as essential and peculiar a feature. There are not, and can never have been, paired-limbed vertebrata without visceral-arch jaws; consequently, wherever the converse is the case, we feel certain that the absence of limbs is a secondarily produced feature. This may serve as an example of admitting certain fundamental characters which may not be applicable to all the members of the group in question.

Various features which we are accustomed to associate with the description of the recent members of a class, order, or family—for instance, the intestinal spiral valve of Plagiostomi—have not been mentioned; partly on account of our imperfect knowledge of the fossil forms, partly because these features do not apply to such fossils which are undoubtedly not only closely allied to, but ancestral to the same group in question. On the other hand, it would be pedantic to exclude all soft, perishable parts on the plea that they are unknown in the fossil forms. Here discretion is to be used. We do not "know" that the palaeozoic Fishes did possess an entirely venous heart, nor has it yet been shown that the embryos of Dinosaurs were surrounded by an amnion; but we feel nevertheless certain, because of the laws of correlation which comparative anatomy allows us to deduct from the study of recent creatures. On the other hand, it is quite possible, even most likely, that the triassic Pseudosuchia, p. 19, had no copulatory organ, and therefore this feature cannot be admitted into the diagnosis of Crocodilia, at least not if they are to comprise the Pseudo-, Para-, and Eusuchia.

The various characters employed are, of course, not all equivalent. The same character, which in some groups is scarcely of more than generic value, runs perhaps through all the members of another class.

The groups into which we are used to combine the animals of the various classes are not, and cannot be, all equivalent. The least objectionable, or rather the most generally accepted "orders," are those of the Mammalia, and it is well understood that the ornithologists' "orders" are of far less morphological value, while the time-honoured "orders" of Reptilia are of infinitely greater importance.

Each class has, so to say, its own standard units, just as one nation reckons with £ s. d., another with dollars and cents, and a third with Mark and Pfennige, which again are not the same as francs and centimes. However, to mitigate the discrepancies as much as possible, and chiefly owing to the bewildering mass of fossil reptiles which have come to light, I have arranged the reptiles in numerous sub-classes, and these again in orders, while for the host of Fishes, "divisions," and for the Birds "divisions," and "legions" have been resorted to as intermediate groups between sub-classes and orders. It is obvious that a class which consists of 10,000 recent species may call for more sub-dividing than one which comprises scarcely one-third of that number.

After all, the practical aim of our classifications is sorting and grouping; the ideal aim is that the system should be a condensed expression of the phylogeny of the creatures dealt with. There are many, and there will be still more classifications, all artificial and dependent upon the taxonomic value which we happen to attribute to the various organs. But there can be only one true or natural system, namely, that which expresses every degree of affinity or descent of every creature which has ever lived or is still living. To that gigantic system, however, no classification will be applicable. Each horizon will require its own classification, with its necessarily arbitrary boundaries.

The living forms are like the growing plants in a peat bog. The latter are more or less separated by intervening stretches of water into patches, islands, and little continents. A foot or two lower down, or if the water-level sinks, the patches change in extent and in numbers, some still remaining apparently separate ("very old, generalised, isolated groups"), but after all connected by the peat, the entangled mass of countless generations.

The sequence of the groups, although arranged as much as possible in ascending order, is of necessity as unnatural as that of the maps in an atlas.

Concerning the generic names, I have been as conservative as possible, using those which we are familiar with in treatises of general zoology and comparative anatomy. The book which speaks of Molge, Tiliqua, Procavia, and Morunga, but does not know Triton, Cyclodus, Hyrax, and Trichechus, has fort-

not yet been written, and this little work is meant to be used by the present generation.

In the arrangement of the recent Amphibia and Reptiles I have followed Mr. G. A. Boulenger, who has given me also many hints concerning the extinct forms. To Professor W. F. R. Weldon I am indebted for numerous criticisms of the whole plan of this work. It must, however, be distinctly understood that neither of my friends can in any way be held responsible for any mistakes or errors of judgment which may be found in this Classification of Vertebrata.

H. GADOW.

CAMBRIDGE.
28th June 1898.

PHYLUM VERTEBRATA
SUB-PHYLUM ACRANIA
SUB-PHYLUM CRANIOTA

   Super-CLASS CYCLOSTOMATA
      CLASS MYXINOIDES
      CLASS PETROMYZONTES
   Super-CLASS HYPOSTOMATA
      CLASS HETEROSTRACA
      ,,   OSTEOSTRACA
      ,,   ANTIARCHA
   Super-CLASS GNATHOSTOMATA
      CLASS ICHTHYES
        I. Sub-CLASS PISCES
          Division *ELASMOBRANCHII*
            Order **Proselachii**
            ,,   **Plagiostomi**
                SELACHII
                RAIAE
          Division *ACANTHODI*
            ,,   *HOLOCEPHALI*
            ,,   *TELEOSTOMI*
          Order **Crossopterygii**

Order **Actinopterygii**
    CHONDROSTEI
    HOLOSTEI
    TELEOSTEI
      PHYSOSTOMI
      PHYSOCLYSTI
      PLECTOGNATHI
      LOPHOBRANCHII

II. Sub-CLASS DIPNOI
  Order **Arthrodira**
    „   **Sirenoidei**

CLASS AMPHIBIA
I. Sub-CLASS PHRACTAMPHIBIA
STEGOCEPHALI
  Order **Lepospondyli**
    BRANCHIOSAURI
    MICROSAURI
    AISTOPODES
  Order **Temnospondyli**
    „   **Stereospondyli**

II. Sub-CLASS LISSAMPHIBIA
  Order **Urodela**
    „   **Apoda**
    Anura
      PHANEROGLOSSA
        ARCIFERA
        FIRMISTERNIA
      AGLOSSA

CLASS REPTILIA
  I. Sub-CLASS PROREPTILIA
  II.   „   PROSAURIA

Order **Lepospondyli**
„ **Stereospondyli**
    PROTOROSAURI
    RHYNCHOCEPHALI

III. Sub-CLASS THEROMORPHA

Order **Anomodontia**
„ **Theriodontia**
„ **Pareiosauria**
„ **Placodontia**

IV. Sub-CLASS CROCODILIA

Order **Pseudosuchia**
„ **Parasuchia**
„ **Eusuchia**

V. Sub-CLASS CHELONIA

Order **Thecophora**
    CRYPTODIRA
    PLEURODIRA
    TRIONYCHOIDEA

Order **Atheca**

VI. Sub-CLASS DINOSAURIA

Order **Sauropoda**
„ **Theropoda**
„ **Orthopoda**
    STEGOSAURI
    ORNITHOPODA

Order **Ceratopsia**

VII. Sub-CLASS PTEROSAURIA
    PTERODACTYLI
    PTERANODONTES

VIII. Sub-CLASS PLESIOSAURIA

Order **Mesosauri**
 „ **Nothosauri**
 „ **Plesiosauri**

IX. Sub-CLASS ICHTHYOSAURIA ✓

X. Sub-CLASS PYTHONOMORPHA ✓

Order **Dolichosauri**
 „ **Mosasauri**

XI. Sub-CLASS SAURIA ✓

Order **Eusauri** ✓

GECKONES ✓
LACERTAE ✓
CHAMAELEONTES ✓

Order **Ophidia** ✓

CLASS AVES

Sub-CLASS ARCHAEORNITHES ✓

Sub-CLASS NEORNITHES ✓

Division *RATITAE* ✓
 „ *ODONTOLCAE* ✓
 „ *CARINATAE* ✓

1. LEGION
COLYMBOMORPHAE
- **Ichthyornithes**
- **Colymbiformes**
  - COLYMBI
  - PODICIPEDES
- **Sphenisciformes** — SPHENISCI
- **Procellariiformes** — PROCELLARIAE

2. LEGION
PELARGOMORPHAE
- **Ciconiiformes**
  - STEGANOPODES
  - ARDEAE
  - CICONIAE
  - PHOENICOPTERI
- **Anseriformes**
  - ANSERES
  - PALAMEDEAE
- **Falconiformes**
  - CATHARTAE
  - ACCIPITRES

3. LEGION *ALECTOROMORPHAE*	Tinamiformes	TINAMI
	Galliformes	MESITES
		TURNICES
		GALLI
		OPISTHOCOMI
	Gruiformes	
	Charadriiformes	LIMICOLAE
		LARI
		PTEROCLES
		COLUMBAE
4. LEGION *CORACIOMORPHAE*	Cuculiformes	CUCULI
		PSITTACI
	Coraciiformes	CORACIAE
		STRIGES
		CAPRIMULGI
		CYPSELI
		COLII
		TROGONES
		PICI
	Passeriformes	ANISOMYODAE
		DIACROMYODAE

CLASS MAMMALIA

    I. Sub-CLASS **PROTOTHERIA** ✓

        Order **Allotheria**

          „   **Monotremata** ✓   *mesozoic mammalia*

    II. Sub-CLASS **METATHERIA** or **MARSUPIALIA** ✓

        Order **Polyprotodontia** ✓

            PROTODONTA

            TRICONODONTA

            TRITUBERCULATA

        Order **Diprotodontia** ✓

    III. Sub-CLASS **EUTHERIA** or **PLACENTALIA** ✓

        Order **Edentata** ✓

            E. NOMARTHRA

            E. XENARTHRA

Order **Trogontia**
    TILLODONTIA
    TYPOTHERIA
    RODENTIA

Order **Cetacea**
    ARCHAEOCETI
    ODONTOCETI
    MYSTACOCETI

Order **Sirenia**
  „ **Ungulata**
    HYRACOIDEA
    TOXODONTIA
    AMBLYPODA
    PROBOSCIDEA
    CONDYLARTHRA
    LITOPTERNA
    PERISSODACTYLA
    ANCYLOPODA
    ARTIODACTYLA
        BUNODONTA
        SELENODONTA s. *RUMINANTIA*

Order **Carnivora**
    CREODONTA
    FISSIPEDIA
    PINNIPEDIA

Order **Insectivora**
    I. VERA
    I. DERMOPTERA

Order **Chiroptera**

Order **Primates** ✔
    LEMURES ✔
    TARSII ✔
    SIMIAE ✔
      PLATYRHINAE
      ARCTOPITHECI
      CATARHINAE
        Cercopithecidae
        Anthropoidae

PHYLUM VERTEBRATA

Bilateral symmetrical animals with segmentally arranged mesoderm, with a central solid axis (Chorda dorsalis, extending through the whole length of the body, from head to tail, hence *holochordate*), dorsally of which lies the tubular central nervous-system, ventrally the gut; the respiratory organs arise from the anterior portion of the gut.

SUB-PHYLUM ACRANIA

LEPTOCARDIA, Mueller = ACRANIA, Haeckel = CEPHALOCHORDA, Balfour

Chorda persistent; without cartilage in the skeletogenous layer. Monorhinal.

Respiratory gut with a permanent hypobranchial groove or endostyle.

Liver a hollow blind-sac. Kidneys represented by metameric nephridia.

Gonads consisting of numerous gonomeres.

With a large peribranchial cavity, or atrium, into which open numerous gill-clefts and nephridia.

No skull, no vertebrae, ribs or other arches, jaws or limbs.

Amphioxus, Yarrel. With right- and left-sided gonads. Five species in European, West-Indian, Californian and Malay seas.

Epigonichthys, Peters. With right-sided gonads only. Three species in seas of Tasmania, Torres Straits, and Ceylon.

Asymmetron, Andrews. With right-sided gonads only. Two species, Bahamas, Louisiades, and Loyalty Islands.

SUB-PHYLUM CRANIOTA

With cartilaginous (unless ossified) cranium, arches and blocks of the axial skeleton.

Super-CLASS CYCLOSTOMATA

CYCLOSTOMATA, Richards = MARSIPOBRANCHII, Bonaparte = MONORHINA, Haeckel

Without visceral arches transformed into jaws, and without paired limbs.

Nasal tube unpaired, median.
Liver a compact gland.
Pronephros persistent.   Gonomeres fused.
With bag-shaped gill-pouches or gill-slits.
Mouth suctorial.

I. CLASS MYXINOIDES

= HYPEROTRETA, Mueller

The Myxinoids are the lowest living true vertebrates. Their hypophysial duct still communicates with the mouth-cavity, and this communicates with the unpaired rhinal opening. If the latter condition is the primitive one, then Fuerbringer (1897) is justified in establishing for the Myxinoids the term "Distoma," creatures which still possess the palaeostoma *and* the neostoma of Kupffer.

The segmental nephric ducts remain separate, and open separately into the long, lateral archinephric ducts.

Ear with one semicircular canal only.—Marine, parasitic.

Bdellostomidae.   Gill-pouches with separate external and internal openings.

Bdellostoma, Heptatrema, Polytrema.

Myxinidae.   The external openings of the gill-pouches are produced into long canals with one posterior opening.

Myxine, Gastrobranchus.

II. CLASS PETROMYZONTES
= HYPEROARTIA, Mueller

Nasal sac not communicating with the mouth-cavity.

The gill-pouches combine internally into one canal, which is situated below the oesophagus, and opens into the mouth-cavity.

Ear with two semicircular canals.—Cosmopolitan.

Petromyzon, Linné. In Europe: P. marinus, P. fluviatilis, P. planeri.

Here probably also:—

Palaeospondylus gunni. Traquair, 1890. Old Red Sandstone of Caithness.

Super-CLASS HYPOSTOMATA

Under the name of Hypostomata I separate the OSTRACODERMI, Cope, as a group equivalent to and intermediate between Cyclo- and Gnathostomata.

Craniota without "limbs" and without jaws. Vertebral column acentrous. With strongly developed dermal skeleton.

I. CLASS HETEROSTRACI, Lankester

Without paired appendages. Trunk and tail with rhomboid scales and fish-like. Skeleton with calcifications, but without bone and without enamel.

Pteraspis. Lower Old Red Sandstone, England.

II. CLASS OSTEOSTRACI, Lankester

Without paired appendages. Calcifications, with bone corpuscles, with or without enamel.

Cephalaspis. Lower Old Red Sandstone, Europe and Canada. Even already in the Ludlow strata, uppermost Silurian.

Auchenaspis. Upper Silurian of Oesel, Eastern Baltic.

III. CLASS ANTIARCHA, Smith Woodward

With bone corpuscles, and with "ganoine." One pair of paddle-like appendages, covered with plates.

Asterolepis. Devonian, Russia.

Pterichthys. Lower Old Red of Scotland, Germany, Russia. Possibly also in the upper Silurian strata of the Eastern Baltic.

Super-CLASS GNATHOSTOMATA, Haeckel

With visceral arches, one pair of which is modified into jaws.

With an anterior and a posterior pair of limbs.

Amphirhinal.

I. CLASS ICHTHYES

Anamnia. Anallantoidea. With fin-limbs. The median fins are supported by skeletal elements.

1. Sub-CLASS PISCES

Respiring by gills only. Heart entirely venous. Nasal blind-sacs not communicating with the mouth.

I. Division—*ELASMOBRANCHI*, Bonaparte. With seven, six, or mostly five, pairs of branchial arches, enclosing as many gill-clefts. The gill-bearing clefts are separated by complete septa, which are continuous with the outer skin.

Vertebrae with chorda-centra, unless still acentrous.

Without membrane bones. Skin with numerous small enamelled denticles.

Males with a pair of mixopterygia.

1. Order **Proselachii**. Mouth subterminal, without a rostrum.

With archipterygium biseriale.

Vertebrae still acentrous.

Pleuracanthus (Xenacanthus) Decheni. Lower Permian and Carboniferous.

Cladodus. Lower Carboniferous. Fins with almost preserial archipterygium.

2. Order **Plagiostomi**, Duméril. Mouth transverse and ventral, with a rostrum.

With Ichthyopterygium preseriale.

Pectoral fins separated from the head.

1. Sub-order SELACHII. Numerous since the Carboniferous mountain Limestone.

0 membrane bones. { dermal plates in Myxacanthus
{ crushell. teeth like . in Chimaera
holostylic
callerid derm plate scales
heterdal sheath with cart muscum . Calcified rings .
na t. dipthy cercal tail .
int durs al fin with spine
teeth with broad triters .
Sensory canals groove like . broadly succulated.
nasal capsule opens into mouth .

Chlamydoselache anguineus, approaching the Proselachii. Japan, Azores, Norway.

Heptanchus, Hexanchus, Pristis, Scyllium, Mustelus, Galeus, Squatina, Zygaena, Cestracion, etc.

2. Sub-order RAIAE. Pectoral fins fused with and surrounding the sides of the head.

Beginning clearly in the Jurassic strata.

Raia, Trygon, Myliobates, Torpedo, etc.

II. Division—*ACANTHODI*, Agassiz. With five Elasmobranch gill-clefts, but each with an external fringe-flap. Mouth sub-terminal.

Vertebrae acentrous.—Without mixipterygia.

Paired and median fins with a strong dermal spine.

Large dermal bones on the jaws; dermal armature of trunk and cranium consisting of small granules.

Acanthodes. From Devonian to Permian, Europe.

Upper Devonian: pelvic fins almost as large as the pectorals, and placed midway between pectorals and anal fin.

Lower Carboniferous: pelvics reduced in size.

Upper Carboniferous: pelvics much reduced, and placed far forwards towards the enlarged pectorals.

Lower Permian: pelvics insignificant; pectorals enormous, and closely approximated towards each other.

Chiracanthus. Old Red, Scotland; both fins well developed.

Diplacanthus. Old Red, Scotland; with clavicle and cleithrum.

III. Division—*HOLOCEPHALI*, Mueller. Palato-quadrate bar fused with the cranium.

Vertebrae acentrous; numerous calcified rings in the notochordal sheath.

Agreeing with Elasmobranchi: males with mixipterygia; absence of membrane bones; conus arteriosus with three series of valves.

Agreeing with Tectobranchi: four gill-clefts, with one large operculum; the gill-septa are thin and incomplete, no longer reaching the surface; with a few large teeth resembling those of Dipnoi; mouth subterminal.

Ptyctodus. Devonian.

Squaloraia. Lower Lias, England.
Chimaeropsis and Myriacanthus. Jurassic, Europe.
Ischyodus, from Jurassic to upper Cretaceous, England.
Callorhynchus antarcticus. Southern seas; the genus known already from the lower Greensand of New Zealand.
Chimaera monstrosa. Seas of Northern hemisphere; Pliocene, Tuscany.
[Ichthyodorylites, Buckland. Enamelled spines of the dermal armour, chiefly from the dorsal fins, of various fishes.
Onchus. Upper Silurian of Ludlow, and lower Devonian.
Homacanthus. Devonian and upwards.
Ctenacanthus. Lower Carboniferous.]

IV. Division — *TELEOSTOMI*, Bonaparte. Vertebrae acentrous or arcocentrous.
Without mixipterygia.
Tectobranchi, *i.e.* gills with one large operculum.
With membrane bones. Mouth terminal or subterminal.
Ova numerous and small.

1. Order **Crossopterygii**,[1] Huxley. Paired fins lobate, with a thick axis and biserial fin-rays. With a pair of jugular plates.

Osteolepis, Diplopterus. Lower Devonian, Europe.
Holoptychius, Glyptolepis. Devonian, Europe and North America.
Megalichthys. Carboniferous, British.
Coelacanthidae, with a large ossified air-bladder; from lower Carboniferous to upper Chalk; Undina, Jurassic; Macropoma, Cretaceous.
Polypterus. African rivers.
Calamoichthys. West African rivers.

2. Order **Actinopterygii**, Cope. Paired fins, with multi-basal, uni-preserial ichthyopterygium.

[1] The Ganoidei of Bonaparte and most other authors comprise the present Crossopterygii, Chondrostei, and Holostei. They can be defined as follows: conus arteriosus with many valves; optic nerves forming a chiasma; with intestinal spiral valve.

1. Sub-order CHONDROSTEI, Mueller. Internal skeleton cartilaginous; vertebrae acentrous.
>   Cheirolepis. Lower Devonian, Scotland.
>   Amblypterus. Lower Permian, Europe.
>   Palaeoniscus, Platysomus. Upper Permian, Europe.
>   Chondrosteus. Jurassic and Cretaceous.
>   - Acipenser. Periarctic, marine and fresh-water; the genus known from the London Clay.
>   - Scaphirhynchus. Mississippi and Central Asia.
>   - Polyodon. Mississippi, Yang-tse-kiang and Ho-ang-ho; known also from the Eocene.

2. Sub-order HOLOSTEI, Mueller. Skeleton osseous.

The following genera (Smith Woodward's Protospondyli) constitute perhaps an older group. Vertebrae with a tendency to form pre- and postcentra.
>   Intestine, with a spiral valve.
>   Lepidotus. Lias to Wealden.
>   Pycnodus. Jurassic to Eocene.
>   Caturus, Eurycormus, Callopterus, Osteorhachis. Jurassic.
>   Euthynotus. Lias.
>   Megalurus. Jurassic.
>   Amia. Lower Miocene of England; A. calva. Recent, in lakes and rivers of Eastern U.S.A.

The following genera (Woodward's Aetheospondyli) possess typical arcocentrous vertebrae and, in the Jurassic forms, with pre- and postcentra alternating; spiral valve vestigial.
>   Aspidorhynchus. Jurassic.
>   Belonostomus. Jurassic and Cretaceous.
>   Lepidosteus. Since lower Eocene of England; L. osseus, recent in U.S.A.

3. Sub-order TELEOSTEI, Mueller. Optic nerves decussating. Without intestinal spiral valve. Heart with a bulbus and no conus (the latter vestigial in Buthyrinus). Skeleton osseous; vertebrae typically arcocentrous and solid.

a. PHYSOSTOMI, Mueller. Air-bladder, when present, with a duct.
>   Posterior fins abdominal, or absent. Gills pectinate.
>   Dorsal fins with ramified or fissate, flexible spines.

With about 2500 species, which have been grouped into twenty to thirty families.

    a. PH. ABDOMINALES. Posterior fins abdominal.

    Siluridae. Silurus, Synodontis, Malapterurus electricus (Africa), Aspredo.

    Scopelidae. Scopelus.

    Cyprinidae. Cyprinus, Barbus, Gobio, Leuciscus, Tinca, Rhodeus, Abramis, Cobitis.

    Scombresocidae. Scombresox, Belone, Exocoetus.

    Esocidae. Esox, periarctic, fresh-water.

    Mormyridae. Mormyrus, Ethiopian fresh-water.

    Sternoptychidae. Argyropelecus, Chauliodus.

    Salmonidae. Salmo, Osmerus.

    Clupeidae. Clupea, Engraulis, Buthyrinus.

    β. PH. APODES. Without posterior fins.

    Gymnotidae. Gymnotus, tropical American fresh-water.

    Muraenidae. Muraena, Anguilla, Conger.

    b. PHYSOCLYSTI, Gegenbaur. Air-bladder, when present, without a duct in the adult. Gills pectinate.

With about 3000 species, which have been sorted into numerous super-families and still more numerous families.

    a. ACANTHOPTERI, Mueller. Dorsal fins protected by some entire spines. Position of pelvic fins variable.

    Perciformes. Perca, Serranus, Toxotes, Mullus, Sebastes.

    Xiphiiformes. Xiphias.

    Scombriformes. Scomber, Thynnus, Echeneis, Zeus, Trachinus, Lophius, Cottus, Trigla, Dactylopterus.

    Gobiiformes. Cyclopterus, Gobius, Periophthalmus.

    Blenniiformes. Blennius, Anarrhichas, Zoarces.

    Gastrosteiformes. Gastrosteus, Fistularia.

    Channiformes. Channa, Ophiocephalus.

    Labyrinthibranchii. Anabas.

    Taeniiformes. Regalecus.

    β. PHARYNGOGNATHI, Mueller, etc. Right and left lower pharyngeal arches fused with each other.

    Labrus, Scarus, Embiotocus, Ditrema.

    γ. ANACANTHINI, Mueller. Dorsal, anal and pectoral fins unprotected by spines. Pelvic fins removed to a jugular or pectoral position, or lost.

Gadidae. Gadus, Lota, Molva.
Ophidiidae. Fierasfer, Ammodytes.
Pleuronectidae. Pleuronectes, Rhombus, Solea.

c. *PLECTOGNATHI*, Cuvier. Physoclystic; maxillae and premaxillae fused with each other and with the cranium. Gills pectinate, but with a very small opercular opening.

Ostracion, Tetrodon, Diodon, Orthagoriscus.

d. *LOPHOBRANCHII*, Cuvier. Physoclystic; gills in the shape of peculiar bunches under a large operculum with narrow opening.

Syngnathus, Nerophis, Phyllopteryx, Hippocampus.

2. Sub-CLASS DIPNOI, Mueller

With gills and lungs. Heart trilocular, with mixed blood. Nasal ducts lead into the mouth-cavity.

With archipterygium, no mixipterygium. Tectobranch.

Conus with numerous series of valves. Membrane bones.

Teeth and the acentrous but potentially chordocentrous vertebral column much resembling Holocephalous conditions; the same applies to the holostylic arrangement.—Spiral valve.

1. Order **Arthrodira**, Smith Woodward. Strong dermal armour, also on the ventral side.

Paired fins vestigial or absent.

With maxilla and premaxilla, which are toothless.

Teeth on mandible and palatal region.

    Coccosteus. Lower Old Red, Scotland.
    Dinichthys. } Lower Carboniferous, Ohio.
    Titanichthys. }

2. Order **Sirenoidei.** Dermal plates restricted to the head. Trunk with imbricating scales, or "naked."

Paired fins present, archipterygial.

    Dipterus. No distinct maxilla and premaxilla. Jugular plates. Cycloid scales. Old Red, England; Russia.
    Phaneropleuron. Upper Old Red, Scotland.
    Ctenodus. Carboniferous, British.
    Ceratodus. No distinct maxilla and premaxilla. No jugular plates. Cycloid scales. Rhaetic, England and Wuerttemberg; Jurassic, Colorado; Karroo, S. Africa. Recent, Queensland and West Australia. Muschelkalk and Keuper, Europe. Trias, India.
    Protopterus. Recent, Africa.
    Lepidosiren. Recent, South America.

II. CLASS AMPHIBIA, Latreille

Anamnia, Anallantoidea, Tetrapoda.

Median fins, when present, not supported by spinal skeletal elements.

With two occipital condyles, or none.

Vertebrae acentrous, pseudocentrous, or notocentrous.

With lungs, and with gills, at least until metamorphosis.

1. Sub-CLASS PHRACTAMPHIBIA, Haeckel

With a considerable amount of bony dermal armour.

√ *STEGOCEPHALI*, Cope. Cranial roof with dermal bones, containing amongst others, two supraoccipitalia, two postorbitalia, two supratemporalia; with interparietal foramen; with three bony pectoro-jugal plates. Tailed.

Carboniferous, Permian, and Triassic epochs.

1. Order **Lepospondyli**, Zittel. Pseudocentrous.
    1. Sub-order BRANCHIOSAURI, Zittel. With gills.
        Branchiosaurus. Lower Red Sandstone, Europe.
    2. Sub-order MICROSAURI, Dawson. Without gills.
        Keraterpeton, Urocordylus. Carboniferous of Nova Scotia.
    3. Sub-order AISTOPODES, Miall. Without limbs and without pectoral girdles.
        Dolichosoma, Ophiderpeton. Carboniferous of Ireland and Bohemia.
2. Order **Temnospondyli**, Zittel. The component units of the vertebrae remain in a separate, unfused state.
    Chelydosaurus. Lower Red, Bohemia.
    Sphenosaurus. Lower Red, Bohemia.

Trimerorhachis. Permian, Texas.
Archegosaurus. Lower Red, Germany.
Actinodon. } Lower Red, France.
Euchirosaurus.

3. Order **Stereospondyli**, Zittel.
Trematosaurus. New Red, Germany.
Capitosaurus. New Red, Germany.
Mastodonsaurus. Trias, Germany, England.
Labyrinthodon. Keuper, England.

2. Sub-CLASS LISSAMPHIBIA, Haeckel

Without bony dermal armour; without supratemporalia, supraoccipitalia, and postorbitalia.

1. Order **Urodela**, Duméril. Pseudocentrous, with the tail remaining throughout life.

Normally with two pairs of limbs. Ilio-sacral attachment acetabular. Skin naked and smooth.

Periarctic, but extending into North-western South America. Fossils unknown until the mid-Tertiary epoch.

Salamandridae. Without gills in the perfect state. Maxillaries present. Both jaws toothed. Eyelids present.

Salamandra. Western palaearctic.
Chioglossa. Iberian peninsula.
Triton. Periarctic.

Amblystoma. Numerous species in North America and Mexico; the larva or "Axolotl" has been described as Siredon. One species, A. persimile, from mountains of Siam.

Allied genera, *e.g.* Ranidens, Salamandrella in Japan, Manchuria, Eastern Siberia.

Plethodon. North America.
Spelerpes. North America, Mexico, Columbia, Costa Rica, Hayti, and North Italy.
Desmognathus. North America.

Amphiumidae. No gills in the perfect state, but with or without a pair of gill-clefts. Maxillaries present. Both jaws toothed. No eyelids.

Cryptobranchus japonicus. Japan, China; without spiracle. Miocene, Europe: Andrias.

Menopoma alleghaniense. Mississippi basin; with spiracle.

Amphiuma means. SE. United States; with spiracle.

Proteidae. External gills persistent. Maxillaries absent. Premaxillaries and mandible toothed. No eyelids.

Necturus = Menobranchus maculatus, in North America. Proteus anguinus, in Carniola.

Sirenidae. External gills persistent. Maxillaries absent. Jaws toothless. No eyelids.

Siren lacertina. South-eastern United States.

Pseudobranchus striatus. Georgia.

2. Order **Apoda,** Oppel. Pseudocentrous. Tail extremely short. Limbs and girdles absent. Skin covered by numerous imbricating concealed dermal scales, which are arranged in rings.

Coeciliidae. About twenty-five species in tropical countries. Palaeotropical and neotropical.

Ichthyophis. Indian and Malayan.

Coecilia. Neotropical. Other genera in South America and in Africa, excluding Madagascar.

3. Order **Anura,** Duméril. Notocentrous. Caudal vertebrae transformed into a coccyx during metamorphosis. Ilio-sacral connexion extremely preacetabular. Fore- and hind-limbs always well developed.

1. Sub-order PHANEROGLOSSA, Wagler. With a tongue. Eustachian tubes opening separately at the base of the cranium. Larva with one spiracle only, either on the left side (majority) or median (Discoglossidae).

a. ARCIFERA, Cope. Distal portions of the coracoids and precoracoids connected with each other by a cartilaginous arch, and that of the one side overlapping that of the other.

1. *Cystignathidae.* Upper jaw toothed. Diapophyses of sacral vertebrae cylindrical or slightly dilated.

Terminal phalanges not claw-shaped. Procoelous, no ribs Arboreal, aquatic, terrestrial, or burrowing.

Neotropical and Australian. Numerous genera, *e.g.*—

Pseudis. South America.

Hylodes. Tropical America.

Ceratophrys. South America.

Chiroleptes. Australia.

2. *Dendrophryniscidae.* No maxillary teeth. Sacral diapophyses not dilated.

Peru. Two species only.

3. *Bufonidae.* Maxillary teeth present. Sacral diapophyses dilated. Procoelous, no ribs.

Terrestrial, arboreal, aquatic, burrowing.

<u>Bufo</u> and several other genera. Bufo is cosmopolitan, with the exception of the Australian region.

Myobatrachus, one species, and Pseudophryne, two species, are the only Australian representatives of this otherwise cosmopolitan family.

4. *Hylidae.* Upper jaw toothed. Sacral diapophyses dilated. Terminal phalanges claw-shaped, swollen.

Procoelous, no ribs.

Cosmopolitan.

Acris. U.S.A.

Hyla. Cosmopolitan, excluding Africa and Madagascar.

Nototrema. Tropical America.

5. *Amphignathodontidae.* Both jaws toothed. Sacral diapophyses dilated. Closely allied to Hylidae.

One species, in Ecuador.

6. *Pelobatidae.* Upper jaw toothed. Sacral diapophyses strongly dilated. No ribs. Terminal phalanges simple. Vertebrae variable.

Pelobates. Europe.

Pelodytes. W. Europe.

Other small genera in North America, Central America, India, Malaya, New Guinea.

7. *Discoglossidae.* Upper jaw toothed. Sacral diapophyses dilated. With short movable ribs.

Opisthocoelous. In tadpoles the spiracle is placed mesially on the thoracic region.

Discoglossus. S. Europe and NW. Africa.

Bombinator. Europe and Asia.

Liopelma. New Zealand. [The only Amphibian in New Zealand.]

Alytes. Western Europe.

8. *Hemiphractidae.* Both jaws toothed. Sacral diapophyses not dilated. Opisthocoelous.

Coracoids and precoracoids not overlapping, nor fused with those of the other side.

A few species in S. America.

ᵛ *b. FIRMISTERNIA*, Cope. Coracoids firmly united with each other.

9. *Ranidae*, Bonaparte. Upper jaw toothed. Sacral diapophyses cylindrical, or very slightly dilated. Procoelous. Without ribs. Since the Miocene.

    Rana. Cosmopolitan, excluding Patagonia, New Zealand and Australia; but one species in Cape York peninsula.
    Rhacophorus and numerous other genera, chiefly palaeotropical; few neotropical, none periarctic.

10. *Dendrobatidae*. No teeth; otherwise like the Neotropical Ranidae.

    Dendrobates. Tropical America.
    Mantella. Madagascar.

11. *Engystomatidae*. Maxilla toothless. Sacral diapophyses dilated. Procoelous, without ribs.

Numerous genera, almost entirely palaeotropical and neotropical.

    Rhinoderma. Chili.

12. *Dyscophidae*. Upper jaw toothed, otherwise like the previous family.

A few species in Madagascar and India.

2. Sub-order AGLOSSA, Wagler. Probably a heterogeneous group of degraded forms specialised by absolutely aquatic life.

No tongue. Eustachian tubes united medioventrally. Larva with two symmetrical spiracles.

No tympanum. Opisthocoelous, epichordal vertebrae.

Shoulder-girdle of the arciferous type, but the two halves do not overlap. Sacral diapophyses strongly dilated.

1. *Xenopidae*. Upper jaw toothed, with a long, epipubic cartilage; unique.

    Xenopus. Ethiopian.

2. *Pipidae*. No teeth.

    Pipa americana. Guiana.

III. CLASS REPTILIA

Amniota.   Allantoidea.   Tetrapoda.
Occipital condyle triple or single.   Vertebrae gastrocentrous.
Ilio-sacral connexion postacetabular.
With lungs only; gills absent.

1. Sub-CLASS PROREPTILIA

Temnospondylous: the three pairs of component units of the vertebrae remain separate; amphicoelous.

    Eryops.   Permian, Texas.
    Cricotus.   Permian, Texas.

2. Sub-CLASS PROSAURIA

Amphicoelous, with intercentra, or with movable chevrons.
Sphenodon, the only recent genus, has no copulatory organs.

1. Order **Lepospondyli**.   Chorda persistent, without interruption.   Ribs with capitulum and tuberculum.

    Hylonomus.   Carboniferous, Nova Scotia.
    Hyloplesion.   Carboniferous, Bohemia.
    Hylerpeton.   Carboniferous, Nova Scotia.
    ?Smilerpeton.   Carboniferous, Nova Scotia.

2. Order **Stereospondyli**.   Centra of vertebrae solid.   With numerous intercentra and chevrons.

Ribs without tuberculum.   Humerus with entepicondylar foramen.

Numerous abdominal "rib-like" ossifications.   Quadrate fixed.

Two sacral vertebrae.   Upper and lower temporal arch.

1. Sub-order PROTOROSAURI, Seeley.   Protorosaurus.   Permian, Germany.

    Palaeohatteria.   Permian, Germany.
    ?Telerpeton.   New Red, Elgin Sandstone.
    ?Simaedosaurus.   Lower Eocene, France, Belgium.

2. Sub-order RHYNCHOCEPHALI, Guenther.
Rhynchosaurus. Keuper, England.
Hyperodapedon. Keuper, England; India.
Homoeosaurus. Upper Jura, Germany.
Sphenodon. New Zealand.

3. Sub-CLASS THEROMORPHA, Cope

Stereospondylous, amphicoelous. Pubes and ischia fused together.
Humerus with entepicondylar foramen. Quadrate fixed.
Ribs with capitulum and tuberculum.
Pentadactyle walking limbs.

1. Order **Anomodontia**, Owen. Walking limbs. Sacrum with five to six vertebrae.
Triple occipital condyle. Without intercentra.
Teeth absent, or restricted to one pair of upper tusks.
    Oudenodon. L. Trias, S. Africa; Permian, Ural?
    Dicynodon. L. Trias, S. Africa; Bengal; Elgin.

2. Order **Theriodontia**, Owen, s. **Pelycosauri**, Cope. With intercentra. Two or three sacrals.
Mostly with differentiated incisors, canines, and molars.
Triple occipital condyle.
    Lycosaurus. Trias, South Africa.
    Cynodraco. Trias, South Africa.
    Galesaurus. Trias, South Africa.
    Clepsydros. Trias, U.S.A.
    Dimetrodon. Trias, U.S.A.

3. Order **Pareiosauri**, Zittel. Teeth in uniform series. Two sacrals. With triple occipital condyle. Caudal intercentra.
    Pareiosaurus. L. Trias, South Africa.
    Elginia. L. Trias, Elgin.

4. Order **Placodontia**, von Meyer. Skull only known. Palate with large, broad teeth. Marine, European.
    Placodus. Muschelkalk, Germany.

4. Sub-CLASS CROCODILIA, Wagler

Stereospondylous. Quadrate fixed. Ribs with capitulum and tuberculum. Two sacral vertebrae. Pentadactyle walk-

ing limbs. Both jaws with numerous alveolar teeth. With "abdominal" ribs. Humerus without entepicondylar foramen. Pubes and ischia distally not united. Pubes simple.

At least with two rows of dorsal dermal bones.

Tail long, with numerous movable chevrons.

In the recent forms: cloacal opening longitudinal; penis anterior, single.

1. Order **Pseudosuchia**, Zittel. Premaxillae separated by the large nasals.

Nares latero-terminal. Without lateral temporal foramen.
    Aetosaurus. Upper Keuper, Wuerttemberg.
    Ornithosuchus. L. Trias, Elgin.

2. Order **Parasuchia**, Huxley. Premaxillae long and united.

Nares far back, near the orbits. Choanae near the anterior end of the separated palatina. With upper and lateral temporal foramen.
    Belodon. Keuper of Europe, India.

3. Order **Eusuchia**, Huxley. Premaxillae short. Nares terminal. Choanae behind the palatine symphysis.

Amphicoelous until the lower Chalk, then procoelous.
    Teleosaurus. Jurassic, since Lias; marine, Europe.
    Steneosaurus. Jurassic, since Lias; marine, Europe.
    Metriorhynchus. Jurassic, since Lias; marine, Europe.
    Pholidosaurus. Wealden and lower Chalk; Europe.
    Gavialosuchus. Miocene, marine, Europe.
    Tomistoma. Miocene, marine, Mediterranean.
    T. schlegeli. Recent, fresh-water, Borneo.
    Gavialis. Pliocene, fluviatile, Siwaliks.
    G. gangeticus. Recent, India, Burmah.
    Alligator. Since the upper Chalk, fluviatile, of Europe. Recent, SE. United States, and China.
    Caiman. East Andean South America.
    Osteolaemus. West African estuaries.
    Crocodilus. Since the upper Chalk of Europe; Tertiary of Europe and North America.

Recent: Africa, India, Austro-Malaya, tropical America (South America, Central America, and Antilles).

Total number of recent Crocodilian species about twenty.

5. Sub-CLASS CHELONIA, Brogniart

Stereospondylous. Quadrate fixed. Ribs with capitulum only. Two sacral vertebrae. Pentadactyle walking limbs or paddles. Both jaws without teeth, but with horny sheaths. Humerus without entepicondylar foramen. Pubes and ischia forming symphyses.

Numerous dorsal and ventral dermal bones, forming a carapace and a plastron.

Cloacal opening longitudinal. Penis anterior, single.

1. Order **Thecophora**, Dollo. Dorsal vertebrae and ribs fused with the dermal plates which form a carapace. With a parieto-pterygoidal column.

1. Sub-order CRYPTODIRA, Duméril. Neck, if retractile, bending in an S-shaped curve in a vertical plane. Pelvis not anchylosed with carapace or plastron.

Chelydridae. Pubic and ischiadic symphyses widely separated from each other. Plastron narrow, cruciform, without entoplastral plate. Tail long.

Since Upper Jurassic of Europe and North America.

Recent: Chelydra serpentina; Macroclemmys temmincki. U.S.A.

Dermatemydidae. Pubic and ischiadic symphyses widely separate. With entoplastral. Short tail.

Dermatemys. America, since Eocene.

Cinosternidae. Pubic and ischiadic symphyses in contact. Without entoplastral.

Cinosternum in Central and North America.

Platysternidae. Pubic and ischiadic symphyses connected by ligament. With entoplastral. Unique character: jugal completely enclosed by postfrontal, maxillae and quadrato-jugal.

Platysternum megacephalum. South China to Siam.

Testudinidae. Pubic and ischiadic symphyses firmly connected with each other. With entoplastron.

Since Eocene: Clemmys and Emys.
Since Miocene: Testudo.

Colossochelys atlas. Upper Miocene, Sivaliks.

Recent distribution of Testudinidae cosmopolitan, with the exception of the Australian region.

Chelonidae. Limbs transformed into paddles. With squamoso-parietal suture. Marine.

Since upper Chalk in Europe and North America.

Recent: Chelone and Thalassochelys.

2. Sub-order PLEURODIRA, Duméril. Neck bending laterally. Pelvis anchylosed with plastron and carapace.

Here possibly Proganochelys. Rhaetic, Wuerttemberg.

Pelomedusidae. With eleven plastrals. Recent, Africa, Madagascar, South America.

?Plesiochelys. Upper Jurassic, Switzerland.

Chelydidae. With nine plastrals. Recent: Chelys fimbriata = matamata; Hydraspis and Hydromedusa. South America.

Chelodina. Australian region.

Carettochelydidae. Limbs transformed into paddles. Without epidermal shields. With nine plastrals.

Carettochelys insculpta. New Guinea.

3. Sub-order TRIONYCHOIDEA, Bonaparte. Neck bending in an S-shaped curve in a vertical plane. Pelvis not anchylosed. With nine plastrals. With three claws. Without epidermal shields. Since the upper Chalk in N. America; Eocene in Europe and U.S.A.

Recent: Trionyx in Asia, Africa, North America.

2. Order **Athecae**, Cope. *Sphargidae.* Dorsal vertebrae and ribs not fused with the carapace, which consists of numerous polygonal plates. Pelvis not anchylosed. Without parieto-pterygoid column. Limbs transformed into paddles. Skin leathery, without epidermal shields. Marine. Potentially cryptodirous.

?Psephoderma. Rhaetic, Bavaria.
Protostega gigas. Upper Chalk, U.S.A.
Protosphargis. Upper Chalk, Venetia.
Eosphargis. London Clay.
Psephophorus. Oligocene, Europe.

Recent: Sphargis (Dermatochelys) coriacea. Intertropical.
Total number of recent Chelonian species about 200.

6. Sub-CLASS DINOSAURIA, Pictet

Stereospondylous. Quadrate fixed. Ribs with capitulum and tuberculum. Limbs terrestrial. With distal ischiadic syndesmosis. Ilium horizontally elongated. With sternum.
Upper Triassic, Jurassic, and Cretaceous.

1. Order **Sauropoda**, Marsh. Pubes simple, with symphysis. Premaxilla with teeth. Fore- and hind-limbs pentadactyle, plantigrade.

> Atlantosaurus, Brontosaurus, Morosaurus, Diplodocus: mostly gigantic beasts of the Upper Jurassic of Wyoming.
> Ornithopsis. Wealden, England.

2. Order **Theropoda**, Marsh. Pubes simple, with symphysis. Premaxilla with teeth. Carnivorous. Fore-limbs shorter than hind-limbs. Metatarsals elongated. Digitigrade.

> Anchisaurus. Upper Trias, Connecticut.
> Brontozoum (Ornithichnites). Connecticut.
> Zanclodon. Keuper, Wuerttemberg.
> Megalosaurus. Oolite, Europe and Colorado.
> Allosaurus, Ceratosaurus, Coelurus, Hallopus. Upper Jurassic, U.S.A.
> Compsognathus. Oolite, Bavaria; hind-limb almost typically avine.

3. Order **Orthopoda**, Cope. Each pubis consisting of an anterior (prepubis) and a posterior (postpubis) arm, without symphyses.

Premaxilla without teeth, and with a predentary edentulous piece. Herbivorous.

1. Sub-order STEGOSAURI, Marsh. Plantigrade. With dermal armour.

> Scelidosaurus. Lias to Chalk, England.
> Stegosaurus. Jurassic, North America.

2. Sub-order ORNITHOPODA, Marsh. Fore-limbs much shorter than hind-limbs, but stout and with five fingers. Hind-limbs elongated, digitigrade.

> Camptosaurus and Laosaurus. Upper Jurassic, U.S.A.
> Hypselophodon. Wealden, England.
> Iguanodon. Wealden, Europe.

Hadrosaurus and Diclonius. Upper Cretaceous, U.S.A.
?Ornithomimus. Upper Cretaceous, Colorado.

4. Order **Ceratopsia**, Marsh. Pubes simple, with symphysis. Pentadactyle, quadrupedous. Maxilla and mandible with a toothless rostrale and predentale. With dermal armour.

Ceratops and Triceratops. Cretaceous, Europe and U.S.A.

7. Sub-CLASS PTEROSAURIA, Kaup

Stereospondylous. Quadrate fixed. Anterior limbs transformed into wings, the enormously elongated ulnar finger carrying the patagium.

1. Sub-order PTERODACTYLI. With alveolar teeth.

   Dimorphodon. Lias, England.
   Pterodactylus and Rhamphorhynchus. Upper Jurassic, Europe.
   Ornithocheirus. Cretaceous, England.

2. Sub-order PTERANODONTES. Without teeth. Scapula articulating with spinous processes of dorsal vertebrae.

   Pteranodon. Cretaceous, Kansas.

8. Sub-CLASS PLESIOSAURIA, Fitzinger

Quadrate fixed. Alveolar teeth. Thoracic ribs without tuberculum. Strong abdominal ribs. One or more sacral vertebrae. No sternum. Neck mostly long. Aquatic.

1. Order **Mesosauri**, Boulenger. Pentadactyle, not more than five phalanges. Vertebrae with persistent notochordal canal. Four sacral vertebrae.

   Mesosaurus. Trias, S. Africa and Brazil.

2. Order **Nothosauri**, Boulenger. Pentadactyle walking and swimming limbs, with not more than five phalanges. Vertebrae solid.

   Nothosaurus. Muschelkalk, Germany.
   Lariosaurus. Upper Trias, fresh water, Lombardy.

3. Order **Plesiosauri**. Limbs transformed into hyperphalangeal paddles. Vertebrae solid. Europe, from the Rhaetic to the upper Chalk, Marine.

   Plesiosaurus, Pliosaurus, Polyptychodon.

9. Sub-CLASS ICHTHYOSAURIA, Geoffroy

Quadrate fixed. Vertebrae deeply amphicoelous. Teeth in one groove, or absent. Ribs with capitulum and tuberculum. No sternum. Strong abdominal ribs. Neck short. Marine. Limbs transformed into hyperphalangeal paddles. Without sacrum.

    Mixosaurus. Muschelkalk, Europe, Spitzbergen.
    Ichthyosaurus. Jurassic and Cretaceous, Europe; Cretaceous, Queensland and New Zealand.
    Baptanodon. Toothless. Jurassic, Wyoming.
    Ophthalmosaurus. Teeth rudimentary. Upper Jurassic and Cretaceous, England.

10. Sub-CLASS PYTHONOMORPHA, Cope

Long-necked with snake-like body, marine. Anterior and posterior limbs pentadactyle.

Acrodont teeth on jaws and pterygoids.

With interparietal foramen.

Pectoral and pelvic girdles, and sternum present.

  1. Order **Dolichosauri**. Mandibles with sutural symphysis. With two sacral vertebrae.

    Acteosaurus. Lower Chalk, Istria.
    Dolichosaurus. Upper Chalk, England.
    ? Plioplatecarpus. Upper Chalk, Holland.

  2. Order **Mosasauri**. Mandibles with ligamentous connexion. Without sacrum. Limbs transformed into paddles. Upper Chalk.

    Mosasaurus. Europe and U.S.A.
    Liodon. N. America, Europe, New Zealand.
    Platecarpus. N. America, New Zealand.
    Clidastes. North America.

11. Sub-CLASS SAURIA, Brogniart

Quadrate movable, except in the degraded, burrowing families of Autosauri. Cloacal opening transverse, penes postero-lateral, double.—Since the cretaceous epoch.

  1. Order **Autosauri**, Haeckel. Right and left mandible

with sutural symphysis. Pectoral girdle at least vestigial, except in the degraded families, 13-17.

1. Sub-order GECKONES, Spix. Lepospondylous. With columella cranii. Sternum, girdles and limbs complete. Ribs prolonged ventrally across into abdominal ribs. Cosmopolitan, warmer zones. About 270 species.

Geckonidae. Amphicoelous; parietal bones distinct.

Gecko, Teratoscincus, etc.

Uroplatidae. Amphicoelous; parietal single.

Uroplates in Madagascar.

Eublepharidae. Probably a heterogeneous group. Procoelous; parietals fused into one.

West Africa, Central America, Indo-Persia.

Eublepharis, etc.

2. Sub-order LACERTAE, Spix. Stereospondylous, procoelous. With columella cranii, except in most of the burrowing, degraded families. Cosmopolitan. About 1300 recent species.

1. *Agamidae.* Acrodont; without supratemporal arch; without osteoderms. Tongue thick and short. With postorbital and postfronto-squamosal arches. Limbs well developed. Asia and SE. Europe, Africa excluding Madagascar, Australian region.

Calotes, Draco, Agama, Chlamydosaurus, Uromastix, Moloch, etc.

2. *Iguanidae.* Pleurodont, without supratemporal arch; without osteoderms on body. Tongue thick.

With postorbital and postfrontal arches. Limbs well developed.

America, Madagascar, Fiji, and Friendly Islands.

Anolis, Basiliscus, Polychrus, Iguana, Phrynosoma.

Amblyrhynchus. Galapagos; algivorous.

Chalarodon and Hoplurus in Madagascar.

Brachylophus. Fiji and Friendly Islands.

3. *Xenosauridae.* Differs from Iguanidae by the teeth not being hollow at base, and by the anterior part of the tongue being retractile.

Xenosaurus grandis. Mexico.

4. *Zonuridae.* Like the Iguanidae, but the supratemporal fossa is roofed over by dermal bones. Distinguished

from Lacertidae by the simple non-retractile tongue. Limbs variable. South and tropical Africa and Madagascar.

Zonurus, with osteoderms covering the body.

Chamaesaura, serpentiform, limbs vestigial.

5. *Anguidae.* Pleurodont, teeth curved and solid. Body with osteoderms; head with all three arches. Anterior part of tongue retractile. Eyelids movable. Limbs variable. With an azygos "occipital" shield. North and South America; European and Mediterranean; transgangetic India.

Gerrhonotus, with limbs.

Ophisaurus (Pseudopus) and Anguis, without limbs.

6. *Helodermatidae.* The pleurodont teeth are grooved in front and behind. Numerous lower labial, poisonous glands. Postorbital arch strong, the others absent. Anterior portion of tongue bifid, protractile. Osteoderms slightly developed.

Heloderma. Mexico.

7. *Varanidae.* Pleurodont. Postorbital arch incomplete. Tongue deeply bifid and protractile. Limbs well developed. No osteoderms.

Varanus in Africa, Asia, Australia.

8. *Xanthusiidae.* Pleurodont. All three arches present. No osteoderms. Eyelids not movable.

Xanthusia, etc. Central America and Cuba.

9. *Tejidae.* No supratemporal arch; no osteoderms. Tongue long and bifid. Teeth pleuro- to acrodont. Limbs variable. America.

Teius, Ameiva, etc.

10. *Lacertidae.* Pleurodont. All three arches present. No osteoderms on the body. Proper eyelids. Tongue bifid retractile.

Lacerta, etc. Palaearctic and Palaeotropical, excluding Madagascar.

11. *Gerrhosauridae.* Pleurodont. All three arches present. Osteoderms strongly developed. Tongue bifid. Limbs variable. Mostly with a lateral fold.

Africa south of the Sahara, and Madagascar.

Gerrhosaurus, Zonosaurus, etc.

12. *Scincidae.* Pleurodont. All three arches present. Osteoderms strongly developed. Premaxilla double. Tongue

nicked feebly. No lateral fold. Limbs variable. Eyelids well developed. Cosmopolitan.

Cyclodus (Tiliqua), Scincus, Trachysaurus, etc. Eumeces

The following five families are composed of degraded forms of various descent, leading mostly a burrowing, subterraneous life. Limbs entirely absent, or the posterior pair reduced to small flaps; girdles correspondingly reduced. Without postorbital, postfronto-squamosal, and supratemporal arches. Body snake-shaped or worm-like.

13. *Anelytropidae.* Degraded Skinks. Teeth hook-shaped. Osteoderms present. Eyes and ears concealed. No limbs. Premaxilla single.

Africa and Mexico.

Anelytropsis in Mexico. Feylinia and Typhlosaurus in Africa.

14. *Dibamidae.* Degraded Skinks. Premaxilla double. No columella cranii. No limbs, except the males, in which the hind-limbs are represented by a pair of flaps on the side of the anus. Eyes and ears concealed. Teeth hook-shaped. Body worm-like. With cycloid imbricating scales.

Dibamus in New Guinea, Moluccas, Celebes, Nicobars.

15. *Aniellidae.* Degraded Anguidae; see Family No. 5. No limbs. Premaxilla single. No squamosal bone. No columella cranii. Eyes and ears concealed. Body snake-like.

Aniella in California.

16. *Amphisbaenidae.* Fore-limbs only or no limbs at all. No columella cranii. Eyes and ears concealed. Pleuro- or acrodont. Worm-like with annular skin-segments.

America including Antilles, Africa, Mediterranean countries.

Chirotes, Blanus, Amphisbaena, Trogonophis, etc.

17. *Pygopodidae.* Pleurodont. Premaxilla single. Hind-limbs reduced to short pentactyle flaps; fore-limbs absent. Body scaly without osteoderms. Eyes open, without movable lids.

Australia and New Guinea.

Pygopus, Lialis, etc.

3. Sub-order CHAMAELEONTES, Wiegmann. Stereospondylous. Procoelous. Without columella cranii. No tympanum. Acrodont. Limbs well developed, fingers and toes arranged in opposing, grasping bundles of two and three.

Tail prehensile. Tongue very long and protractile. Palaeo-tropical.

Only Family *Chamaeleontidae.* Only genus, with two subgenera: Chamaeleon. About fifty species, almost all in the Malagasy sub-region and in Africa; two species in South Arabia and Socotra; one in India and Ceylon.

2. Order **Ophidia**, Brogniart. Right and left mandible with loose ligamentous connexion.

Without sternum and pectoral limbs and girdle.

Pelvic limbs and girdle absent or vestigial.

About 1600 recent species.

The oldest known Ophidian is Palaeophis, London Clay, England.

Typhlopidae. Pelvis vestigial. Mandible with coronoid. Without ectopterygoid. Pterygoid not articulating with the quadrate. Owing to absence of the squamosal, the quadrate articulates directly with the prootic. Prefrontal in contact with nasal. Eyes hidden by shields. Burrowing snakes. Maxilla very short, loose, toothed. Mandible toothless.

  Typhlops. South Europe, South Asia, Africa, Australia, South America.

Glauconiidae. Like the Typhlopidae, but maxilla fixed and toothless, mandible toothed. With vestige of femur.

  Glauconia. Africa, SW. Asia, tropical America.

Boidae. Both jaws toothed. With ectopterygoid, supratemporal and coronoid. With vestigial pelvis and hind-limbs. Prefrontal in contact with nasals. Supratemporal large and loose.

  Boa, Python, etc. Cosmopolitan.

Ilysiidae. Like the Boidae, but the supratemporal is small and firmly wedged in between quadrate and prootic.

  Ilysia in Guiana. Cylindrophis in Indo-Malaya.

Uropeltidae. Both jaws toothed. With coronoid. Prefrontal in contact with nasal. Without supratemporal, and without vestiges of limbs and pelvis.

Small burrowing snakes of Southern India.

  Uropeltis, Rhinophis, etc.

Colubridae. Both jaws toothed. With movable supratemporal bone. Prefrontals not reaching the nasals. No coronoid. Maxilla horizontal. Pterygoid articulating with quadrate.

a. Aglypha. Teeth solid, not grooved. Cosmopolitan.
    Tropidonotus, Zamenis, Coluber, Dendrophis, Coronella, Calamaria, Dasypeltis (Rhachiodon), etc.

b. Opisthoglypha. One or more of the posterior maxillary teeth are grooved. Slightly poisonous. Cosmopolitan.
    Psammophis, Dryophis, etc. Hypsirhina (entirely aquatic and viviparous).

c. Proteroglypha. Anterior maxillary teeth grooved or perforated. Very poisonous.

Tail cylindrical, terrestrial; mostly viviparous, cosmopolitan, warmer zones.
    Elaps, Naja, Bungarus, Sepedon, Dendraspis, etc.

Tail laterally compressed; aquatic, viviparous.

Indian and Pacific coasts. Hydrophis, etc.
    Distira, landlocked in fresh-water lake of Luzon.

Amblycephalidae. Like the Colubridae, but pterygoid short and not reaching quadrate; supratemporal vestigial. Aglyphodont. Neotropical and Indo-Malayan.
    Amblycephalus, etc.

Viperidae. With movable supratemporal, pterygoid articulating with quadrate. Maxilla short and vertically erectile to the pterygoid. No coronoid. Prefrontal not in contact with nasal. Viviparous, excluding Atractaspis. Very poisonous. Cosmopolitan, excluding Madagascar and Australia.

Viperinae. Maxilla solid. No pit on the side of the snout. Europe, Asia, Africa.
    Vipera, Cerastes, Echis, Atractaspis, etc.

Crotalinae. Maxilla hollowed out above, receiving the deep, externally visible pit.
    Ancistrodon. Asia, America.
    Lachesis. SE. Asia and S. America.
    Crotalus. America. *Sistrurus*

IV. CLASS AVES, Linné

Warmblooded, oviparous, Amniota, Allantoidea. Occipital condyle single. Quadrate movable. Anterior extremities transformed into wings. Covered with feathers. With intertarsal joint. Not more than four toes, of which the first is the hallux. Total number of recent species nearly 10,000, of which about half are Oscines.

1. Sub-CLASS ARCHAEORNITHES (Carus), Gadow

The three fingers and their metacarpals (I, II, III) remain separate, each with a claw. Well developed remiges. Both jaws with alveolar teeth.

Amphicoelous. Caudal vertebrae more than thirteen, without a pygostyle, but with paired rectrices.

Archaeopteryx. Oolite, Bavaria.

2. Sub-CLASS NEORNITHES, Gadow

Metacarpals fused. Second finger the longest.
Not more than thirteen caudal vertebrae.

1. Division—*NEORNITHES RATITAE*, Merrem. Terrestrial, flightless. Without sternal keel. Quadrate with single proximal knob. Without pygostyle. Coracoid and scapula fused. No pterylae. Compound rhamphotheca. With copulatory organ.

A collective cosmopolitan group; with certainty since the Miocene.

? Diatryma. Eocene, New Mexico.
? Gastornis, Dasornis. Eocene, Europe.

1. *Struthiones*, Wagler. Two toes (3rd and 4th). With symphysis pubis; unique in birds.
> Struthio. Africa and Arabia; Miocene of Samos; Pliocene, Sivalik Hills.

2. *Rheae.* Three toes. With long ischiadic symphysis!
> Rhea. Neotropical.
> Mesembriornis. Miocene or Pliocene, Argentina.

3. *Casuarii*, Kaup. Three toes. Aftershaft as long as the other half.
> Casuarius, Dromaeus. Australian region.
> Hypselornis. Pliocene, Sivalik Hills.

4. *Apteryges.* Four toes. Long, slender bill.
> Apteryx. New Zealand.

5. *Dinornithes.* Three or four toes. Bill short. Anterior extremities extremely reduced.
> Dinornis. Numerous species, recently extinct. New Zealand.

6. *Aepyornithes.* Four toes.
> Aepyornis. Recently extinct. Madagascar.

2. Division—*NEORNITHES ODONTOLCAE*, Marsh. Marine, flightless, without sternal keel.' Teeth in furrows. Cretaceous.
> Enaliornis. England; vertebrae chiefly biconcave.
> Hesperornis. U.S.A.; vertebrae heterocoelous.

3. Division—*NEORNITHES CARINATAE*, Merrem. With keeled sternum.

1. Order **Ichthyornithes**. Vertebrae amphicoelous. Teeth alveolar. With small pygostyle. With incisura ischiadica. Cretaceous of Kansas.
> Ichthyornis, Apatornis.

2. Order **Colymbiformes**. Plantigrade, nidifugous, aquatic. Fourth toe largest, hallux short; all toes webbed. Metatarsus laterally compressed with high, pyramidal epicnemial crest. Bill straight, pointed, with simple sheath.

1. Sub-order COLYMBI. Front toes completely webbed. Patella much reduced.
> Colymbus. Periarctic.

2. Sub-order PODICIPEDES. Toes lobated. Patella absent.

Podicipes. Cosmopolitan, excluding Arctic and Antarctic.
Centropelma. Titicaca lake; flightless.

3. Order **Sphenisciformes**. Nidicolous, marine; flightless, wings transformed into rowing paddles.

SPHENISCI. Coasts of antarctic and southern temperate countries, and Galapagos.

Palaeeudyptes. Oligocene, New Zealand.
Palaeospheniscus. Eocene, Patagonia.
Spheniscus, Eudyptes, and Aptenodytes.

4. Order **Procellariiformes**. Well-flying, pelagic, nidicolous; hallux absent or vestigial. Rhamphotheca compound. Cosmopolitan.

Sub-order PROCELLARIAE s. TUBINARES. Diomedea, Oceanites.

Procellaria, Puffinus, Prion, etc. Oceanites.

5. Order **Ciconiiformes**. Swimmers or waders; desmognathous, without basipterygoid processes. With one pair of sternotracheal muscles.

1. Sub-order STEGANOPODES, Illiger. Well-flying, aquatic, nidicolous, with all the four toes webbed together. Cosmopolitan.

Phaetontidae. Phaeton.
Sulidae. Sula, since Miocene.
Phalacrocoracidae. Phalacrocorax, since Miocene; Plotus.
Fregatidae. Fregata, Tachypetes.
Pelecanidae. Since Miocene.

Pelagornis, Miocene, France; Argillornis, Eocene, England.
Odontopteryx toliapicus. Eocene, England.

2. Sub-order ARDEAE, Wagler. Piscivorous, nidicolous waders, with complicated hypotarsus, and with long cervical apteria. Cosmopolitan.

Ardeidae. Ardea, since Miocene; Cancroma, Balaeniceps.
Scopidae. Scopus Afra.

Proherodius. Eocene, England.

3. Sub-order CICONIAE. Carnivorous, nidicolous waders, with simple hypotarsus, and with cervical apteria. Cosmopolitan.

Ciconiidae. Ciconia, Abdimia, Leptoptilus, etc.
Ibidae. Ibis, Platalea.

Propelargus. Oligocene.

4. Sub-order PHOENICOPTERI. Nidifugous. Very long legs and neck; front toes completely webbed.

Phoenicopterus. Cosmopolitan; since Miocene.
Elornis, Palaelodus. Oligocene, Europe.

6. Order **Anseriformes**. Desmognathous, nidicolous, with two pairs of sterno-tracheal muscles, with complete basipterygoid processes and with a penis.

1. Sub-order PALAMEDEAE. Without uncinate processes on the ribs.

Quadrate with two proximal articular knobs.
Hypotarsus simple.
Neotropical: Palamedea, Chauna.

2. Sub-order ANSERES. Hypotarsus complex. Basipterygoid processes articulating near the anterior ends of the pterygoids. Cosmopolitan.

Only Family *Anatidae*. Anas, Anser, Cygnus, etc. Since Miocene.

Cnemiornis. Plistocene, New Zealand; flightless.

7. Order **Falconiformes**. Desmognathous, nidicolous, carnivorous, terrestrial, without functional caeca.

1. Sub-order CATHARTAE. With nares perviae. American.
Only Family *Cathartidae*. Cathartes, Catharistes.

2. Sub-order ACCIPITRES. With nares imperviae. Cosmopolitan.

Gypogeranidae. Gypogeranus. Ethiopian.
Vulturidae. From Portugal to Siam, and to South Africa.
Falconidae. Gypaetus; Aquila since Oligocene, Falco, Pandion.

Harpagornis. Plistocene, New Zealand.
Lithornis. Eocene, England.

8. Order **Tinamiformes**. Nidifugous, with incisura ischiadica, without pygostyle. Neotropical.

Sub-order TINAMI. *Crypturidae*. Tinamus s. Crypturus, Rhynchotus, Nothura, etc.

9. Order **Galliformes**. Terrestrial, schizognathous; with ten functional remiges. With strong spinae sterni (either spina interna, eventually sp. communis, and in this case without basipterygoid processes, or only with a strong spina externa and with basipterygoid processes).

1. Sub-order MESITES. Without basipterygoid processes, and with large spina interna.

    Mesites variegatus. Madagascar.

2. Sub-order TURNICES. Nidifugous; vomer large, sternum without processus obliqui. Hallux absent or vestigial. Old World.

    Turnicidae. Quintocubital. Hallux absent.

        Turnix *s.* Hemipodius. S. Europe, Africa, India.

    Pedionomidae. Pedionomus. Australia.

3. Sub-order GALLI. With large spina communis sterni and large processus obliquus. Hallux functional.

    Megapodiidae. Australian and Austro-Malayan. Megapodius, Talegallus, Megacephalon, etc.

    Cracidae. Neotropical, excluding Antilles: Crax, Penelope, Ortalida, etc.

    Gallidae. Cosmopolitan. Meleagris, Numida; Tetrao, Ortyx; Perdix, Francolinus, Coturnix, etc.; Gallus, Phasianus, Pavo, Argus.

4. Sub-order OPISTHOCOMI. Arboreal. With long spina externa sterni; without basipterygoid processes.

    Ophisthocomus cristatus. Guiana and Venezuela.

10. Order **Gruiformes.** Legs of the "wading" type. Without basipterygoid processes. Without spina interna sterni. Essentially schizognathous, excluding Rhinochetus and Dicholophus. Cosmopolitan.

    Rallidae. Cosmopolitan, since Oligocene.

        Rallus, Fulica, Ocydromus, etc.

        Gallinula nesiotis. Tristan d'Acunha; flightless.

        Notornis. New Zealand; flightless, recently extinct.

        Aphanapteryx (Mauritius), = Erythromachus (Rodriguez) = Diaphorapteryx (Chatham Island); flightless and recently extinct.

        Aptornis. Recently extinct: New Zealand; flightless.

        Gypsornis. Upper Eocene, France.

    Gruidae. Cosmopolitan, excluding New Zealand and Pacific. Grus, Aramus; Psophia.

        ? Phororhacos. Tertiary, Patagonia.

    Dicholophidae. Dicholophus *s.* Cariama. Brazil and Argentina.

Otididae. Otis, etc. Old World, since Miocene.
Rhinochetidae. Rhinochetus jubatus. New Caledonia.
Eurypygidae. Eurypyga. Neotropical.
Heliornithidae. Heliornis, Neotropical. Podica, Ethiopian and Indo-China.

11. Order **Charadriiformes**. Schizognathous, with eleven remiges, of which the terminal very short; aquintocubital. Spinae sterni short, separate.

1. Sub-order LIMICOLAE. Nidifugous, schizognathous, without spina interna sterni; hypotarsus complicated. Cosmopolitan.

Charadriidae. Charadrius, Vanellus, Ibidorhynchus, Haematopus, etc.
  Tringa, Phalaropus, Scolopax, Rhynchaea, Numenius, Limosa, etc. Cosmopolitan.
Chionididae. Chionis. Kerguelen Islands.
Glareolidae. Glareola, Cursorius, Dromas. Old World.
Thinocorythidae. Thinocorys, Attagis. South America.
Oedicnemididae. Oedicnemus. Cosmopolitan, excluding North America, Australasia, and New Zealand.
Parridae. Parra. Neotropical, Ethiopian, Malagasic, Indo-Malayan.
  Hydrophasianus. Indian.

2. Sub-order LARI. Aquatic, schizognathous, vomer complete. Without basipterygoid processes. Front toes webbed; hallux small or absent. Large supraorbital glands. Since the Miocene.

Laridae. Nidifugous. Cosmopolitan.
  Lestris, Larus, Sterna, Rhynchops.
Alcidae. Northern half of the periarctic region.
  Alca, Fratercula, etc.

3. Sub-order PTEROCLES. Nidifugous. With large crop and large caeca. Vomer vestigial. Hallux vestigial or absent. From Portugal to India, and to the Cape of Good Hope.

Pteroclidae. Pterocles and Syrrhaptes.

4. Sub-order COLUMBAE. Nidicolous, with large crop, vestigial caeca. Cosmopolitan.

Columbidae. Since Miocene.
  Columba, Treron, Caloenas, Goura, Didunculus.

Dididae. Without basipterygoid processes. Flightless.
Didus ineptus. Mauritius.
Pezophaps solitarius. Rodriguez.

12. Order **Cuculiformes**. Desmognathous; zygodactylous, or with the outer toe reversible; deep flexors of the toes normal (Type I). Nidicolous.

1. Sub-order CUCULI. Zygodactylous, or with outer toe reversible. Quintocubital. Cosmopolitan.

Cuculidae. Cuculus, Coccystes; Phoenicophaes; Centropus, Crotophaga, etc.

Musophagidae. Ethiopian. Musophaga, Corythaix, etc.

2. Sub-order PSITTACI. Zygodactylous. Aquintocubital. Cosmopolitan, chiefly tropical.

Trichoglossidae. Nestor. New Zealand.
Lorius, Trichoglossus, etc.

Psittacidae. Stringops, Cacatua. Lophopsittacus, Mauritius, recently exterminated. Psittacus, Chrysotis, Platycercus, Conurus.

13. Order **Coraciiformes**. Nidicolous; nares imperviae; holorhinal. Downs restricted to the apteria, or absent. Thirteen to fifteen cervical vertebrae. Deep plantar tendons connected with each other. Mostly desmognathous. Cosmopolitan.

1. Sub-order CORACIAE. Either (1) syndactyle, and with long spina externa sterni; without spina interna.
Or (2) eleutherodactyle, and with spina communis.
Or (3) outer toe reversible, and with spina externa only.

Coraciidae. Old world. Leptosoma, Coracias, etc.
Momotidae. Neotropical. Momotus, Todus.
Alcedinidae. Cosmopolitan.
Alcedo, Ceryle, Dacelo, Ceyx, etc.
Meropidae. Old world. Merops, Nyctiornis.
Upupidae. Palaearctic and palaeotropical.
Buceros, Irrisor, Upupa.

2. Sub-order STRIGES. Outer toe reversible. Long functional caeca. Schizognathous. Cosmopolitan.

Strigidae. Strix, Bubo, Asios, Otus, etc.

3. Sub-order CAPRIMULGI. Nocturnal. With gaping mouth. Ten remiges and rectrices. Spinae sterni vestigial. Caeca functional.

Steatornithidae. Steatornis. Peru to Trinidad.
Podargidae. Australia and Papuasia.
  Podargus, Batrachostomus, Nyctibius, etc.
Caprimulgidae. Cosmopolitan.
  Caprimulgus, Chordeiles, etc.

4. Sub-order CYPSELI. The tenth, terminal, remex is the longest. With short spina sterni externa and interna. No caeca.

Cypselidae. Cosmopolitan.
  Cypselus, Chaetura, Collocalia, Dendrochelidon, etc.
Trochilidae. American: Trochilus, Patagona, etc.

5. Sub-order COLII. First and fourth toes reversible.
Coliidae. Ethiopian: Colius.

6. Sub-order TROGONES. Heterodactyle; first and second toes directed forwards; third and fourth backwards. Tropical.
    Trogon and Pharomacrus in America. Hapaloderma in
      Africa. Harpactes in Indo-Malaya.
    Trogon gallicus. Miocene, France.

7. Sub-order PICI. Tendon of the m. flexor hallucis sending a strong vinculum to that of the m. flexor profundus digitorum, the tendon of which goes to the third toe only. Zygodactylous. Neotropical.

Galbulidae. Galbula, Jacamarhalcyon, etc., Bucco, etc.
Capitonidae. Palaeotropical and neotropical.
    Capito, Megalaema, Pogonorhynchus, etc., Indicator.
      Palaeotropical.
Rhamphastidae. Neotropical.
    Rhamphastus, Selenidera, etc.
Picidae. Cosmopolitan excluding Madagascar and Australian regions. Picus, Tiga, Picumnus, etc., Yunx.

14. Order **Passeriformes**. Nidicolous. Aegithognathous, without basipterygoid processes.

Spina externa sterni large, spina interna absent.
Quintocubital. Toes normal.

1. Sub-order PASSERES ANISOMYODAE, Gadow. Indo-Malayan, New Zealand; neotropical and nearctic.

SUBCLAMATORES. Deep plantar flexor tendons, connected by a vinculum.

Eurylaemidae. India and Indo-Malayan.
 Eurylaemus, Psarisomus, Calyptomena, etc.
CLAMATORES. Deep flexor tendons not connected.
Pittidae. Palaeotropical and Papuasian.
 Pitta, Philepitta.
Xenicidae. New Zealand: Xenicus, Acanthidositta.
Tyrannidae. America: Tyrannus, Pipra.
 Cotinga, Rupicola, Chasmorhynchus, etc.
Formicariidae. Neotropical.
 Formicarius, Dendrocolaptes, Furnarius, etc.
Pteroptochidae. Neotropical.
 Conopophaga, Pteroptochus, Hylactes, etc.

2. Sub-order **PASSERES DIACROMYODAE**, Fuerbringer. Hallux strong, with large claw.

SUBOSCINES. Australia.
Menuridae. Menura, Atrichia.
OSCINES. Cosmopolitan. With certainty since the Miocene.

The Oscines, with more than 4500 recent species, are divided into about thirty families, few of which can be defined.
  Corvus, Muscicapa, Turdus, Meliphaga, Drepanis,
   Hirundo, Fringilla, Alauda, etc.

V. CLASS MAMMALIA, Linné

Warm-blooded Amniota, Allantoidea with milk-glands. Covered with hair. Quadrate transformed into the ~~os tympanicum~~; mandible articulating with the squamosal. Two occipital condyles. Ilio-sacral connexion preacetabular. With cruro-tarsal joint.

1. Sub-CLASS PROTOTHERIA, Huxley

Oviparous. With a cloaca. Without chorion.
Temporary marsupium, without nipples.
Coracoids complete and articulating with the sternum.
With large "epipubic or marsupial" bones.
Mandible with (at least vestigial) an inner inverted angle.

1. Order **Allotheria**, Marsh. Molars multitubercular. Small mammals from the Triassic to the Eocene epoch.
— Tritylodon. Trias, S. Africa.
Bolodon. Jurassic, England.
Allodon. Jurassic, Wyoming.
Plagiaulax. Jurassic, England.
Microlestes. Rhaetic, Europe.
Polymastodon. Eocene, New Mexico.

2. Order **Monotremata**, Geoffroy = Ornithodelphia, de Blainville. Multi-tubercular molars are superseded by horny coverings of the jaws. Australian region.
Ornithorhynchus in Australia.
Echidna and Proechidna. Australia and New Guinea; since the Plistocene of Australia.

2. Sub-CLASS METATHERIA, Huxley, s. MAR-
SUPIALIA, Illiger, s. DIDELPHIA, de Blainville.

Viviparous, with marsupium; without chorion; with epipubic or marsupial bones.

Coracoids reduced, not reaching the sternum.

Males at least without cloaca.

1. Order **Polyprotodontia**, Owen. Dentition complete; lower jaw with three or four pairs of incisors. Carnivorous; without caecum. Since the Triassic epoch.

1. Sub-order ?PROTODONTA, Osborn. Dromatherium. *microconed* Upper Trias, Carolina.

2. Sub-order ?TRICONODONTA, Osborn. Amphilestes and Phascolotherium, Oolite; Triconodon, upper Jurassic, England.

3. Sub-order TRITUBERCULATA, Cope.
Amphitheriidae. Jurassic, Cretaceous, England.
Amblotheriidae. Amblotherium and Dryolestes. Jurassic and Cretaceous of North America.
Myrmecobiidae. Myrmecobius fasciatus. West Australia.
Peramelidae. Perameles, Chaeropus. Australia.
Dasyuridae. Dasyurus, Thylacinus. Australia, since the Plistocene.

Doubtful relatives in Tertiary, Patagonia.
Notoryctidae. Notoryctes typhlops. Central Australia.
Didelphyidae. Since the Eocene in America and Europe.
Recent:
Didelphys. N. and S. America.
Chironectes. S. America, Chile.

2. Order **Diprotodontia**, Owen. Lower jaw with one pair of incisors.

Canines weak or absent. Herbivorous, with caecum.

Since the Mid-Tertiary epoch in South America; since the Plistocene in Australia.

Epanorthidae. Epanorthus. Mid-Tertiary, Patagonia.
Caenolestes. Ecuador and Columbia.
Phalangistidae. Phalangista, Petaurus, Phascolarctos, in Australia and Papuasia.

Diprotodontidae. Diprotodon, Notothcrium. Plistocene, Australia.
- *Macropodidae.* Macropus, Hypsiprymnus. Australia.
  Macropristis. Plistocene, Patagonia.
  Thylacoleontidae. Thylacoleo. Plistocene, Australia.
- *Phascolomyidae.* Phascolomys. Since the Plistocene in Australia.

3. Sub-CLASS EUTHERIA, Huxley, s. MONODELPHIA de Blainville, s. PLACENTALIA, Owen

Viviparous, with chorion and placenta. Without marsupium, and without marsupial bones.

Coracoids reduced to the "coracoid process" of the scapula.

Males at least without cloaca; perineum separating the anal and urogenital orifices.

1. Order **Edentata** (Vicq. d'Azyr), Cuvier. Terrestrial. Dentition reduced to molars without enamel, or lost completely.

Probably a heterogeneous assembly.

1. Sub-order NOMARTHRA, Gill. With normal vertebral zygapophyses. Restricted to the Old World.

Orycteropodidae. Orycteropus, now Ethiopian; upper Miocene of Samos.

Manidae. Manis. Palaeotropical; in India since the Oligocene.

2. Sub-order XENARTHRA, Gill. Zygapophyses with additional articular facets. American, since the Oligocene.

Bradypodidae. Bradypus, Choloepus. Central and South America.

Megatheriidae. Extinct, Tertiary.
  Moropus. Miocene, North America.
  Morotherium. Lower Pliocene, North America.
  Mylodon, Scelidotherium. Plistocene of South America.
  Megatherium. Plistocene, America, etc.

Myrmecophagidae. Myrmecophaga, Cycloturus. Neotropical.

Dasypodidae. Neotropical. Recent:
Dasypus, Priodon, Tatusia, Chlamydophorus. Plistocene: Hoplophorus, Glyptodon, etc.

2. Order **Trogontia**, Haeckel. Terrestrial, plantigrade, pentadactyle (unless the first digit is reduced as in some Rodentia).

Clavicles mostly strong.

Tendency of the second pair of incisors to excessive, rodential development, and gradual suppression of the first and third pair of incisors. Canines reduced or lost.

1. Sub-order TILLODONTIA, Marsh. Pentadactyle, with claws. Dentition complete; second incisor largest.

Mandibular condyle transverse.

Humerus with entepicondylar foramen.

Femur with third trochanter.

Lissencephalous. Eocene.

Esthonychidae. Esthonyx. Lower Eocene of North America and England.

Tillotheriidae. Tillotherium. Wyoming.

Stylinodontidae. Stylinodon. North America and Europe.

2. Sub-order TYPOTHERIA, Zittel. Digits $\frac{5}{5 \text{ or } 4}$. One pair of upper incisors enlarged. Molars prismatic, high, mostly rootless. Mandibular condyles roundish. With entepicondylar foramen, and with third trochanter. Tertiary.

Protypotheriidae. Protypotherium. Mid-Tertiary, Patagonia.

Typotheriidae. Typotherium, new Tertiary. Pachyrucos. Tertiary, Patagonia.

✓ 3. Sub-order RODENTIA, Vicq. d'Azyr. Digits $\frac{5 \text{ or } 4}{5, 4 \text{ or } 3}$. Second pair of incisors much enlarged and rootless; the others much reduced or lost. Canines absent. Mandibular condyle longitudinal. Clavicles weak or absent.

Uterus bicornis. Placenta discoid, deciduous. Cosmopolitan, few in Australia and Madagascar. About 900 recent species.

✓ *LAGOMORPHA*, Brandt. Incisors $\frac{2}{1}$; one small incisor is placed behind the much enlarged second. Fibula articulating

with the calcaneum. Tibia and fibula separate. Narrow infraorbital canal.

    Leporidae. Palaeolagos. Lower Miocene, U.S.A.

        Lepus. Since Miocene; cosmopolitan, excluding Australasia.

        Lagomys. Periarctic; since Miocene.

HYSTRICOMORPHA, Brandt. Incisors $\frac{1}{1}$. Wide infraorbital canal. Tibia and fibula separate.

    Hystricidae. Periarctic, Ethiopian, neotropical.

        Hystrix, Erethizon. Since Miocene.

    Dasyproctidae. Neotropical.

        Dasyprocta, Coelogenys, Dinomys.

    Octodontidae. Neotropical.

        Octodon, Myopotamus, Capromys.

        Ethiopian: Aulacodus.

        ?Theriodomys. Eo- and Miocene, Europe.

    Caviidae. Neotropical: Cavia, Hydrochoerus, Dolichotis.

    Chinchillidae. Neotropical: Chinchilla, Lagostomus.

    ?Castoroides. Plistocene. North America and Antilles.

    ?Eocardidae. Tertiary, Patagonia.

SCIUROMORPHA, Brandt. Incisors $\frac{1}{1}$. Infraorbital canal small. Tibia and fibula separate.

    Cosmopolitan, excluding Australian region.

    Sciuridae. Sciurus, Arctomys, Tamias, Pteromys, Haplodon, etc.

        Sciuroides. Eocene, Europe.

    Anomaluridae. Ethiopian: Anomalurus.

    Castoridae. Periarctic, since Miocene: Castor.

MYOMORPHA, Brandt. Incisors $\frac{1}{1}$. Infraorbital canal wide. Tibia and fibula fused. Since the Oligocene. Cosmopolitan.

    Myoxidae. Since Eocene, now palaearctic and Ethiopian.

        Myoxus, Muscardinus.

    Muridae. Cosmopolitan: Mus. Periarctic: Arvicola. Palaearctic and palaeotropical: Gerbillus, etc. Periarctic and neotropical: Cricetus, etc., since Miocene.

        Madagascar: Hypogeomys, Nesomys.

        Australian: Hydromys, Hapalotis.

    Spalacidae. Palaearctic and palaeotropical, excluding Madagascar: Spalax, Rhizomys, Heterocephalus.

Geomyidae. Nearctic and neotropical.
    Geomys, Dipodomys.
Dipodidae. Periarctic and Ethiopian.
    Pedetes, Dipus.
    ?*Ischyromys.* Eo- and Miocene, North America.

3. Order **Cetacea** (Linné), Cuvier. Anterior limbs transformed into paddles; posterior limbs lost. Tail long, with a horizontal fluke.

Teeth, if present, without enamel; monophyodont.

Teats inguinal. Placenta diffuse, non-deciduous. Cosmopolitan. About 150 recent species.

1. Sub-order ARCHAEOCETI, Flower. All the ribs with capitulum and tuberculum.

Posterior teeth two-rooted. Skull symmetrical.
    Zeuglodon. Marine. Eocene of Alabama, Europe and New Zealand?

2. Sub-order ODONTOCETI, Gray. Posterior ribs without capitulum.

All the teeth one-rooted. Skull asymmetrical.

Since the Miocene epoch.

Squalodontidae. Squalodon. Marine, Mid-Tertiary of Europe, North America, Australia.

Platanistidae. Platanista, Ganges.
    Inia, Amazon. Pontoporia, La Plata.

Delphinidae. Since the marine Pliocene, cosmopolitan.
    Delphinus, Phocaena, Orca, Monodon, etc.

Physeteridae. Since the Miocene, marine.
    Physeter, Ziphius, Mesoplodon, etc.

3. Sub-order MYSTACOCETI, Gray. Most ribs without tuberculum.

Teeth absent. Whalebone. Skull symmetrical.

Cosmopolitan, marine, since Miocene.

Balaenidae. Balaena, Balaenoptera, etc.

4. Order **Sirenia**, Illiger. Anterior limbs transformed into paddles, occasionally hyperphalangeal, namely, four phalanges.

Posterior limbs vestigial or lost.

Tail long, with a horizontal fluke.

Teeth with enamel. Teats pectoral.

Placenta zonaris, non-deciduous.

Marine, littoral, since the Eocene period.
Prorastomidae. Prorastomus. Eocene, Jamaica.
Manatidae. Manatus. Atlantic basin, tropical America and Africa.
    Halicoridae. Halitherium. Eocene and Oligocene, Europe.
    Rhytiodus. Miocene, France.
    Felsinotherium. Pliocene, Italy.
    Halicore. Indian Ocean, Africa to Austro-Malaya.
    Rhytina. North Pacific, exterminated in 1768.

✓ 5. Order **Ungulata**, Wagner.

Herbivorous, terrestrial, diphyodont. Without clavicles. Toes encased in hoofs, excluding Hyracoidea.

1. Sub-order HYRACOIDEA. Small, plantigrade, with $\frac{4}{3}$ toes. Carpalia and tarsalia serial. Fibula complete, articulating with the astragalus, not with the calcaneum.

Dentition $\frac{1}{2} \cdot \frac{0}{0} \cdot \frac{4 \cdot 3}{4 \cdot 3}$, incisors rodential.

Placenta zonary, deciduous.—Gut with one sacculated and two conical cacca (unique).

    Hyracidae. Hyrax and Dendrohyrax. Cape to Syria.

2. Sub-order TOXODONTIA, Owen. Semiplantigrade, with $\frac{3}{3}$ toes. Carpalia and tarsalia alternating. Fibula complete, articulating with the calcaneum and astragalus. Some of the upper and lower incisors enlarged.

Tertiary epoch of South America.

    Toxodon, Nesodon; size from that of a sheep to that of a rhinoceros.

3. Sub-order AMBLYPODA, Cope. Semiplantigrade, with $\frac{5}{5}$ toes. Carpalia alternating, tarsalia and metatarsalia serial. Fibula complete, articulating with the astragalus, not with the calcaneum.

Upper canines enlarged.

Eocene epoch of Europe and America.

    Coryphodon. Eocene of England, France, Wyoming, New Mexico.
    Uintatherium (Dinoceras). Eocene of Wyoming.
    Astrapotherium. Patagonia.

4. Sub-order PROBOSCIDEA, Illiger. Semiplantigrade herbivora with $\frac{5}{5}$ toes. Carpalia serial, tarsalia slightly alternating. Fibula complete, articulating with astragalus and calcaneum.

One or two pairs of incisors transformed into tusks, canines absent. With a long proboscis.

Placenta zonary, deciduous. Mammae pectoral.

During the Miocene cosmopolitan, excluding Australia. Now palaeotropical.

Dinotheriidae. No upper incisors, lower pair transformed into down-curved tusks.

Dinotherium. Miocene of Europe and India.

Elephantidae. Mastodon with upper and lower tusks. Miocene and Pliocene of Europe, India, North America; Plistocene of North, Central, and South America.

Elephas, with upper tusks only. Since the upper Miocene in India. Plio- and Plistocene of Asia, Europe, North Africa, North and South America. Recent in Africa, India, Ceylon, Sumatra.

5. Sub-order CONDYLARTHRA, Cope. Plantigrade, with $\frac{5}{5}$ toes. Carpalia serial. Dentition complete. Fibula complete, but not articulating with either calcaneum or astragalus.

Dentition complete.

Eocene of North America and Europe.

Periptychus and Meniscotherium. Lower Eocene, U.S.A.

Phenacodus. Lower Eocene of U.S.A. and Europe.

6. Sub-order LITOPTERNA, Ameghino. Digitigrade. Carpalia and tarsalia serial. Fibula complete, articulating with the calcaneum and astragalus. Feet perissodactyle.

Tertiary epoch of South America.

Macrauchenia. Miocene to Plistocene.

Protherotherium. Eocene and Oligocene.

7. Sub-order PERISSODACTYLA (Cuvier), Owen. Digitigrade. The third toe forms the functional axis. Carpalia and tarsalia alternating.

Fibula, when complete, articulating with the astragalus, not with the calcaneum.

Placenta diffused, non-deciduous. Mammae inguinal. Stomach simple. Caecum large.

Tapiridae. Lower molars with two transverse ridges. Toes $\frac{4}{3}$. Since the Eocene of America and Europe.

Lophiodon. Eocene of Europe.

Heptodon, Helaletes. Eocene of U.S.A.

Ribodon. Oligocene, South America.

Protapirus. Eocene of Europe.

✓ Tapirus. Miocene of Europe and India, recent in Central and South America, Malacca, Sumatra, and Borneo.

Equidae. Lower molars quadritubercular or with two transverse ridges curved into two half-moons, leading to W pattern. Toes $\frac{4}{4}$, $\frac{3}{3}$ or $\frac{1}{1}$. Since the Eocene.

Hyracotherium. ⎱ Toes $\frac{4}{3}$. Lower Eocene, England.
Eohippos. ⎰ Lower Eocene, Wyoming.

Palaeotherium. ⎫
Mesohippos. ⎬ Toes $\frac{3}{3}$. Lower Miocene, Dakota.
Anchitherium. ⎭ Upper Miocene, of Europe = Miohippos, U.S.A.

Eocene to Miocene, Europe and U.S.A.

Hipparion. Toes $\frac{3}{3}$. Upper Miocene of Europe, Asia and U.S.A.

Protohippos. Toes $\frac{3}{3}$. Pliocene, U.S.A.

Pliohippos. Toes $\frac{1}{1}$. Pliocene, U.S.A.

Hippidion. Toes $\frac{1}{1}$. Plistocene, South America.

✓ Equus. Toes $\frac{1}{1}$. Since Miocene in India, since Pliocene in Europe. During the Plistocene cosmopolitan, excluding Australian region.

Rhinocerotidae. Lower molars with two transverse half-moons. Toes $\frac{4 \text{ or } 3}{3}$. Since the Eocene.

Hyrachius. Upper Eocene, Wyoming.

Hyracodon. Lower Miocene, Nebraska.

Aceratherium. Oligocene, France; Miocene, Europe, India, North America.

Diceratherium. Miocene, Oregon.

Rhinoceros. Since the Miocene in Asia, Plistocene of Asia and Europe. Recent in the palaeotropical regions including Sumatra, Java, Borneo, excluding Madagascar.

Titanotheridae. Eocene and Miocene of Europe and North America.

Palaeosyops. Eocene, U.S.A.

Titanotherium (Brontotherium). Lower Miocene, U.S.A.

Leptodon. Upper Miocene, SE. Europe.

8. Sub-order ANCYLOPODA, Cope. Plantigrade; terminal

phalanges strongly curved. Carpalia and tarsalia alternating. Fibula complete, articulating with the calcaneum.

Tertiary epoch:
    Homalodontotherium. Eocene, Patagonia.
    Macrotherium. Miocene, Europe.
    Chalicotherium (Ancylotherium). Upper Miocene of Europe and India.

9. Sub-order ARTIODACTYLA (Cuvier), Owen. Digitigrade. The functional axis passes between the third and fourth toes.

Carpalia and tarsalia alternating.
Fibula articulating with the astragalus and calcaneum.
Placenta diffused or cotyledonary, non-deciduous.
Stomach complex. Caecum small.

A. BUNODONTA, Kowalewsky. Molars tubercular. Carpalia, tarsalia, and metapodials separate. Placenta diffuse.

Suidae. Cosmopolitan, excluding Australian region minus New Guinea.
    Choeropotamus and Cebochoerus. Upper Eocene, Europe.
    Elotherium. Oligocene of Europe and lower Miocene of North America.
    Sus. Since Miocene in Europe. Recent in the palaearctic and Indian regions, and Indo-Malayan islands, including New Guinea.
    Babirusa. Celebes.
    Phacochoerus. Ethiopian, extinct in Madagascar.
    Dicotyles. North and South America.

Hippopotamidae. Hippopotamus. Since the Pliocene in Asia and Europe. Now in the Ethiopian sub-region, recently extinct in Madagascar.

Anthracotheridae. Upper Eocene to Miocene.
    Anthracotherium. Europe and India.
    Hyopotamus. Europe and North America.
    Merycopotamus. India.

Oreodontidae. Eocene to Pliocene of America.
    Protoreodon. Eocene, U.S.A.
    Oreodon. Miocene, U.S.A.
    Diplotremus. Pliocene, South America.

Anoplotheridae. Eocene to lower Miocene of Europe.

Dichobune, Caenotherium, Anoplotherium, Xiphodon.

β. *SELENODONTA*, Kowalewsky, s. *RUMINANTIA*, Vicq. d'Azyr. The tubercles of the molars are transformed into longitudinally placed half-moons. Third and fourth metapodials fused.—Ruminating.

Tragulidae. Placenta diffuse. Since the upper Eocene.
 Gelocus. Upper Eocene, Europe.
 Leptomeryx. Miocene, North America.
 Eoauchenia. Upper Miocene, South America.
 Dorcatherium. Miocene of Europe and India; recent: Tragulus, Malay Islands, Ceylon, and India; Hyaemoschus, West Africa.

Camelidae. Placenta diffuse.
 Poebrotherium, Procamelus. Miocene, U.S.A.
 Auchenia. Since Pliocene in South America.
 Camelus. Since upper Miocene in India, Plistocene in Siberia; recent in Central Asia, introduced into Africa.

Pecora. Placenta with cotyledons.

a. Cervidae[1] s. *Cervicornia.* Frontal bony excrescences, if present, during their growth surrounded by hairy skin which is deciduous.

 a. Without frontal excrescences.
 Until the middle Miocene.
 Recent: Moschus and Hydropotes. Central Asia.

 b. With bony cores, permanently covered with skin.
  Helladotherium and Samotherium. Upper Miocene of South Europe and India.
  Giraffa. Since upper Miocene of South Europe and India; now Ethiopian sub-region.
  Sivatherium. Upper Miocene, Sivalik.

 c. With bony cores or antlers, which are periodically shed; cosmopolitan except African and Australian regions.
  Cervulus. SE. Asia.
  Cervus, Alces, Rangifer, Capreolus.

 d. Bony core permanent, horns deciduous.
  Antilocapra. North America.

β. *Bovidae* s. *Cavicornia.* Males, and most females, with permanent "horns" of epidermal origin, surrounding a bony core.

---

[1] The distinction between *Cervidae* and *Bovidae* is fanciful.

Since the upper Miocene in Europe. Now cosmopolitan except neotropical and Australian regions.

Tetraceros, Gazella, Rupicapra, Capra, Ovis, Ovibos, Bos.

6. Order **Carnivora**, Cuvier. Diphyodont, heterodont; mostly with three, rarely two pairs of upper and lower incisors; canines strong. Mandibular condyle transverse. Toes five, rarely four. Fibula complete and separate. Clavicles vestigial or absent.

Mammae abdominal. Uterus bicornis. Placenta zonaris, deciduous.

1. Sub-order CREODONTA, Cope. Scaphoid and lunar of the carpus separate.

Chiefly Eocene, from the lowest Eocene to the lower Miocene, of North America and Europe.

 Oxyclaenus. New Mexico.
 Arctocyon, etc. Europe and North America.
 Triisodon. New Mexico.
 Mesonyx. North America.
 Proviverra, etc. North America and Europe.
 Palaeonictis, etc. North America and Europe.
 Hyaenodon, etc. North America and Europe.
 Miacis, etc. North America.

2. Sub-order FISSIPEDIA, Flower. Scaphoid fused with the lunar bone. Toes separate.

Ursidae. Ursus since the lower Pliocene of India, now periarctic, Indian, Malayan, Andean.

 Arctotherium. Plistocene of South America and California.
 Hyaenarctos. Miocene of Europe and India.

Procyonidae. Procyon, Cercolaptes, America. Aelurus, Himalayas.

Mustelidae. Cosmopolitan: Lutra, Enhydra; Meles, Mephitis, Mellivora; Mustela, Gulo.

Canidae. Otocyon and Lycaon, Ethiopian. Canis, since the upper Miocene in Europe, now cosmopolitan, excluding Madagascar and Antilles.

Hyaenidae. Hyaena. Pliocene in Europe, now palaeotropical. Proteles, South Africa. ?Ictitherium, lower Pliocene, SE. Europe and India.

Viverridae. Palaearctic and palaeotropical regions.

Viverra since the Eocene; Herpestes, Paradoxurus.

Cryptoprocta. Madagascar.

Felidae. Felis, since the Pliocene epoch, now cosmopolitan excluding Australian region, Madagascar and Antilles. Cynaelurus, from Cape through Persia to South India.

> Machaerodus. Eocene to Plistocene in Europe, Asia, and South America; Smilodon, Plistocene, America. Proaelurus, Pseudaelurus, Nimravus in Miocene of America and Europe.

3. Sub-order PINNIPEDIA, Illiger. Anterior and posterior extremities transformed into paddles, the toes being completely connected by webs. Scaphoid and lunar bones coalesced.

Marine cosmopolitan. Since the upper Miocene.

Phocidae. Chiefly arctic and periarctic seas; landlocked in Lake Baikal and Caspian. Phoca, Cystophora, etc., since Miocene.

Macrorhinus leoninus, Eastern Pacific and Antarctic.

Otariidae. Pacific ocean and southern temperate seas.

Otaria. Since the Pliocene epoch.

Trichecidae. Arctic seas; Plistocene, France.

Trichechus.

7. Order **Insectivora**, Cuvier. Dentition complete, diphyodont, heterodont; not less than two pairs of lower incisors. Plantigrade. Clavicles present.

Placenta discoidal, deciduous.

Cosmopolitan with the exception of the Australian region and the South American continent.

1. Sub-order INSECTIVORA VERA, Flower. Limbs free. Incisors conical.

Tupajidae. Oriental: Tupaja, Ptilocercus.

Macroscelidae. Ethiopian: Macroscelides.

Erinaceidae. Palaearctic and palaeotropical.

Necrogymnurus, Eocene, France. Gymnura, Malayan.

Erinaceus. Since the Miocene; palaearctic, Ethiopian, and cisgangetic Indian.

Soricidae. Periarctic: Sorex. Periarctic and palaeotropical including Madagascar: Crocidura.

Talpidae. Periarctic. Myogale, Europe, since Miocene.

Talpa. Palaearctic since Oligocene. Condylura, Nearctic.

Solenodontidae. Solenodon, Hayti and Cuba.
Chrysochloridae. Ethiopian: Chrysochloris.
Centetidae. Madagascar: Centetes, Oryzoryctes.
Potamogalidae. African region. Potamogale, Ethiopian: Geogale, Madagascar.
? *Ictopsidae.* Eocene, North America.
? *Adapiscoricidae.* Eocene, Europe.

2. Sub-order INSECTIVORA DERMOPTERA, Illiger. Fore- and hind-limbs connected by a parachute. Fingers and toes not elongated, free.

Lower incisors pectinated, upper incisors multicuspid.

Galeopithecidae. Galeopithecus. Indo-China, Malay Islands and Philippines.

8. Order **Chiroptera**, Blumenbach. Anterior limbs transformed into wings, second to fifth fingers elongated and carrying part of the patagium. Mammae pectoral. Placenta discoidal, deciduous. Cosmopolitan.

Pteropodidae. Palaeotropical and Australian regions.

Pteropus, Epomophorus, Notopteris.

Vespertilionidae. Cosmopolitan. Since the Eocene of Europe and North America.

Vespertilio, Vesperugo, Plecotus, Thyroptera, Rhinolophus, Nycteris.

Emballonuridae. Intertropical.

Emballonura, Molossus, Phyllostoma, Vampyrus.

9. Order **Primates**, Linné. Extremities modified into hands and feet.

Heterodont, diphyodont.

Incisors $\frac{2}{2}$, at least in the young.

Orbit surrounded by a complete bony ring.

Clavicles well developed.

Testes scrotal, penis pendent.

1. Sub-order LEMURES, Hubrecht. Orbit posteriorly surrounded by a fronto-jugal arch, but widely communicating with the temporal fossa. Mammae pectoral, excluding Chiromys. Testes scrotal, penis pendent. Placenta non-deciduous, diffuse. Allantois large. Pollex and hallux opposable. Second toe with a pointed claw, other fingers and toes with flat nails.

Lacrymal foramen outside the margin of the orbit.

Fossil Lemurs since the Eocene: Adapis (Caenopithecus), ? Necrolemur (Microchoerus), Plesiadapis, of Europe; Pelycodus (Lemuravus), etc., Wyoming. Now palaeotropical.

Lemuridae. $i\frac{2}{1 \text{ or } 2} c\frac{1}{1} pm\frac{2 \text{ or } 3}{2 \text{ or } 3} m\frac{3}{3}$.

Indris, Propithecus, Lemur, Chirogale. Madagascar.
Galago. African continent.
Loris, Nycticebus. Further India, Sumatra, Java, Borneo.
Perodicticus. West Africa.

Chiromyidae. $i\frac{1}{1} c\frac{0}{0} p\frac{1}{0} m\frac{3}{3}$. Chiromys. Madagascar.

2. Sub-order TARSII. Orbit to a great extent separated from the temporal fossa. Lacrymal foramen outside the orbit. Allantois small. Placenta discoidal, deciduous.

Tarsiidae. $i\frac{2}{1} c\frac{1}{1} p\frac{3}{3} m\frac{3}{3}$.

Tarsius spectrum. Malay Islands and Philippines.

Allied is probably Anaptomorphus from the Eocene of Wyoming and Argentina, with only two premolars, but with still wide temporo-orbital communication.

3. Sub-order SIMIAE, v. d. Hoeven. Orbit completely separated from the temporal fossa by an inward extension of frontal and malar meeting the alisphenoid.

Mammae pectoral. Testes scrotal. Penis pendent.
Placenta discoidal, deciduous. Hallux opposable.

PLATYRHINAE. $Pm\frac{3}{3}, m\frac{3}{3}$. Parietal and malar in contact, separating the frontal from the alisphenoid.

Pollex opposable. Broad internarial septum.
External auditory meatus not bony. Tail mostly prehensile.

Cebidae. Tropical America. Mycetes, Nyctipithecus, Cebus, etc. Since the Plistocene of S. America.

ARCTOPITHECI. $Pm\frac{3}{3}, m\frac{2}{3}$. Parietal and malar in contact. Platyrhine. Pollex not opposable.

Tail not prehensile. External auditory meatus not bony.

Hapalidae. Tropical South America: Hapale.

CATARHINAE. $Pm\frac{2}{2}, m\frac{3}{3}$. Frontal and alisphenoid in contact, separating the parietal from the malar.

Internarial septum narrow, nostrils looking forwards. External auditory meatus bony.

Tail not prehensile.

Cercopithecidae. With a tail, excluding Macacus inuus. Africa and Asia.

Cercopithecus, Cynocephalus, Ethiopian, Pliocene of India. Macacus from Marocco to Japan. Semnopithecus, SE. Asia, Pliocene of India and France.

Miocene of S. Europe : Oreopithecus, Mesopithecus.

Anthropoidae. Caudal vertebrae transformed into a coccyx. Walk erect or semierect.

Hylobates. SE. Asia. " Gibbon."
Pliopithecus. Miocene of Europe.
Simia satyrus, " Orang Utan." Sumatra and Borneo.
Troglodytes gorilla and T. niger. West equatorial Africa.
T. sivalensis. Pliocene, Punjab.
Dryopithecus. Miocene, France.
Pithecanthropus erectus. Plistocene, Java.
Homo sapiens. Cosmopolitan.

GEOGRAPHICAL DISTRIBUTION

NOTOGAEA (Huxley). Southern World

I. Australian region (Sclater).
 1. New Zealand sub-region (Wallace).
 2. Australian sub-region (Wallace).
 3. Papuasian or Austro-Malayan sub-region (Wallace).

II. Neotropical region (Sclater).
 1. South American sub-region.
 2. Antillean or West-Indian sub-region.

ARCTOGAEA (Huxley). Northern World

III. Periarctic region (Gadow) = Holarctic (Heilprin).
 1. Palaearctic sub-region (Sclater).
  a. Eurasian province.
  b. Mediterranean province.
 2. Nearctic sub-region (Sclater).
  a. Canadian province.
  b. Sonoran province.

IV. Palaeotropical region (Gadow).[1]
 1. African sub-region.
  a. Ethiopian province.
  b. Malagasy province.
 2. Oriental sub-region.
  a. Indian province.
  b. Malay province.

---

[1] By the establishment of the Palaeotropical region (Bronn's *Thierreich, Vocyel. Systemat. Theil*, p. 296, 1893), the Ethiopian (African) and the Indian or Oriental regions of Sclater and Wallace assume their proper subordinate rank of sub-regions.

NOTOGAEA

Characterised by Dipnoi; *Cystignathidae*.
Chelydidae, Iguanidae.
    Galli peristeropodes.
Diprotodont marsupials.
Absence of Ganoids, *Cyprinidae*, Viperidae, Vulturidae.

1. AUSTRALIAN REGION. Characteristic features:
All the Anura are "arcifera," with the exception of a few species of Rana in New Guinea and the Cape York peninsula.
All the Chelonians are "pleurodira," viz. Chelydidae.
All the poisonous snakes are Elapidae.
Casuarii, Trichoglossidae, Cacatuinae, Podarginae, Meliphaginae, Paradiseinae, Suboscines. Absence of Pici and Fringillinae.
Monotremata and Marsupialia. Extreme scarcity of placental Mammals; entire absence of Edentata, Insectivora, and Primates; of Ungulata only one species of Sus in New Guinea. Concerning Celebes see p. 57.

  1. NEW ZEALAND SUB-REGION. Characterised by *Sphenodon. Apteryx, Dinornithidae, Stringops, Xenicidae.*
Sole representative of Amphibia is *Liopelma.*
Of Reptilia only Geckos and *Sphenodon.*
Absence of Mammalia, excluding one Bat and Mus maorium.
  2. AUSTRALIAN SUB-REGION. Characterised by *Ceratodus; Monotremata (Echidna* and *Ornithorhynchus), Macropodidae, Notoryctes.*
Casuarii, Megapodiidae, Meliphagidae, Paradiseinae, *Suboscines (Menura* and *Atrichia).*
Of placental mammals occur only: Canis dingo, half a dozen genera of Rodents, e.g. *Hydromys, Xeromys,* Mus, and numerous Chiroptera.
  3. PAPUASIAN or AUSTRO-MALAYAN SUB-REGION. In reality a transitional district of debatable extent between the Oriental and Australian regions. "Wallace's line," between Borneo and Celebes, Java and Lombok, is of little significance.

Note.—Italic type indicates animals which are peculiar to the respective regions or sub-regions.

a. The divisional line is applicable to the following animals :—

Trionychidae. Viperidae. Hooded Elapidae.
Trogones, Cacatuinae, Meliphaginae.
Phalangistidae, Manidae, Rhinoceros, Ursus, Mustelinae, Felis, Hystricinae, Tupajidae, Galeopithecus.

b. The following animals extend eastwards, beyond the line :—

Labyrinth-fishes.
Pelobatidae; Rana and Bufo.
Crocodilus. Crotalinae. Tortricinae.
Treron into Celebes, Timor, and the Moluccas, but not into New Guinea.
Pici into Celebes. Bucerotinae into New Guinea.
Sus into Celebes and New Guinea.
Several Monkeys, Tarsius, Viverra, Paradoxurus, Cervus, *Anoa, Babirusa*.
Sciurus, in Celebes.
Celebes should therefore be excluded from the Austro-Malayan sub-region.

c. The following animals extend westwards, beyond the line :—

Megapodiidae. Ptilinopus.

d. The line is otherwise inapplicable to Paradiseinae and Fringillinae.

4. POLYNESIAN SUB-REGION, better to be treated as a province of the New Zealand sub-region. Characterised rather by absence of terrestrial and fluviatile animals.

Hawaian Islands: one species of Bufo; Geckones, Bats; characterised by *Drepanididae*.

II. NEOTROPICAL REGION. Characterised by Cystignathidae; *Tejidae*, Amphisbaenidae; *Cracidae*.

1. SOUTH AMERICAN SUB-REGION. Characterised by *Lepidosiren*.

Pipa, Dendrobatidae, Hylidae.
Pelomedusidae, Chelydidae, Testudinidae.
Crocodilus and Alligator.
Crotalinae; Amphisbaenidae.

Rhea ; *Palamedea* ; *Tinami* ; *Dicholophus*, *Eurypyga*, Cathartae, *Opisthocomus*, *Rhamphastinae*, Trochilidae.

Edentata *xenarthra* ; Marsupialia (Didelphyidae and *Caenolestes*) ; Camelidae (*Auchenia*, *Llama*) ; Dasyproctidae, Caviidae ; Tapirus, Cariacus ; fossil: *Litopterna* and *Toxodontia* ; *platyrhine* Monkeys and *Arctopitheci*.

Absence of Insectivora, excluding Shrews in Guatemala and Costa Rica.

2. ANTILLEAN or WEST-INDIAN SUB-REGION. Characterised by Hylidae, Boinae, Crotalinae, Crocodilus, Cracidae.

Solenodontidae, Octodontidae.

Absence of Elapidae and Chelydidae ; Marsupialia, Edentata, Ungulata, Carnivora, Primates.

ARCTOGAEA

Characterised by *Ganoidei*, *Cyprinidae*.
Fossil: *Dinosauri*.
Galli alectoropodes.
Abundance of Insectivora and Ungulata.

III. PERIARCTIC REGION. Characterised by Ganoidei, *Acipenser*, Cyprinidae, *Esocidae*, *Freshwater Salmonidae*, *Gasterosteidae*.

Urodela, almost peculiar to the region. Pelobatidae.
Colymbi, *Alcidae*, *Tetrao*, *Lagopus*.
Bison, *Rangifer*, *Cervus*, Ovis, *Castor*, *Lynx*, Ursus, *Talpa*.

Absence of: *Dipnoi*, *Ratitae*, Monotremata, practically of Marsupialia and Edentata, Lemures.

1. PALAEARCTIC SUB-REGION. Characterised by Discoglossidae.

Lacertidae. Viperidae.
Otididae.
Erinaceidae, *Talpa*, *Myogale*, *Rupicapra*, *Capreolus*. Cervus. Alces. Sus.

Absence of Passeres anisomyodae ; Marsupialia, Edentata.

a. EURASIAN PROVINCE. Characterised by Acipenser and Esox ; Tetrao, Castor, Talpa.

b. MEDITERRANEAN PROVINCE. Characterised by absence of the genera mentioned in Eurasian province, and presence

of genera otherwise Ethiopian or Indian; Testudo, Geckones, Viverra, Hyaena, Felis leo, Hyrax.

2. NEARCTIC SUB-REGION. Characterised by *Lepidosteus, Amia,* Polyodon. Urodela.

Chelydridae, Trionychidae, Crotalidae.

Of Ungulata are present only Bos, *Ovibos, Haploceros, Antilocapra,* Cervus, Cariacus, Alces, Dicotyles.

Didelphys. *Condylura.*

Cathartae, *Meleagris,* Tyrannidae.

Absence of Viperidae, Agamidae, Varanidae.

Absence of Otididae, Turnices, Coraciae with the sole exception of a few species of Ceryle (Alcedinidae).

Absence of Sus and Monkeys.

a. *CANADIAN PROVINCE.* Characterised by *Ovibos, Haploceros,* Alces, Rangifer, Cervus, *Condylura.* Trionychidae.

b. *SONORAN PROVINCE.* Characterised by *Antilocapra,* Dicotyles, and considerable influx of otherwise neotropical forms, as Didelphys, Tatusia, Cariacus, Felis concolor.

Alligator, Iguanidae, etc.

IV. PALAEOTROPICAL REGION. Characterised by Crocodiles, Trionychidae, Varanidae, *Chamaeleons, hooded Elapidae,* Ratitae, Trogones, *Bucerotinae,* Upupinae, Treron, Pittidae.

Lemures, catarrhine Monkeys, large Felidae, Hyaenidae, Viverridae, Hystricidae, *Tragulidae, Rhinoceros, Elephas,* Edentata *nomarthra.*

Almost entire absence of Urodela.

1. AFRICAN SUB-REGION. Characterised by Chelydidae, Pelomedusidae, Crocodilus, Chamaeleo.

Hippopotamus, Hyomoschus; Lemures; richness in Ungulata, especially Antilopes, Bovinae, Equus.

Absence of Urodela, *Hylidae,* Pelobatidae, Crotalidae; Cervidae, and Ursidae.

a. *ETHIOPIAN PROVINCE.* Characterised by *Protopterus, Polypterus, Calamoichthys.*

Xenopus.

Amphisbaenidae. Varanidae. Pythonidae.

Struthio, Podica, *Serpentarius, Colii, Musophaginae.*

Orycteropus, Manis, Hyrax, Giraffa, Felis leo, *Gorilla, Troglodytes,* Lemures.

b. MALAGASY PROVINCE. Characterised by Dendrobatidae, abundance of Chamaeleons and Lemurs.

Mesites.

Centetidae, Cryptoprocta ferox.

Absence of Ganoidei, Trionychidae, Amphisbaenidae, Varanidae, Lacertidae, Viperidae, Crotalidae, Elapidae; Bucerotinae, Pici; Ungulata excluding Sus; Hyrax, Felidae, Canidae, Simiae.

2. ORIENTAL SUB-REGION. Characterised by Pelobatidae, Crotalidae, Viperidae, and Elapidae. Crocodilus, *Gavialis.*

Trogones and *Subclamatores,* Pittidae.

Hylobates, Simia, Ursidae, Felis tigris, *Tupajidae,* Manis, *Tragulus,* abundance of Cervidae. Elephas. Rhinoceros.

Absence of Ganoids and Dipnoi. Chamaeleo only in Southern India and Ceylon.

a. INDIAN PROVINCE.

b. MALAY PROVINCE. Characterised by Podica, Tapirus, *Tarsius, Galeopithecus.*

APPROXIMATE NUMBER OF RECENT SPECIES OF VERTEBRATA

Acrania		10
Cyclostomata		17

ICHTHYES

Elasmobranchi	290	
Holocephali	2	
"Ganoidei"	32	
Teleostei	7000	
Dipnoi	4	
		7328

AMPHIBIA

Urodela	100	
Apoda	25	
Anura	800	
		925

REPTILIA

Rhynchocephali	1	
Crocodilia	20	
Chelonia	200	
Autosauri	1620	
Ophidia	1600	
		3441
AVES		9818
MAMMALIA		2702
Total		24,241

AVES

Ratitae	17
Colymbiformes	19
Sphenisci	12
Procellariiformes	90
Ciconiiformes	155
Anseriformes	150
Falconiformes	350
Tinamiformes	35
Galliformes	367
Gruiformes	233
Laro-Limicolae	270
Pteroclo-Columbae	360
Cuculi	200
Psittaci	400
Coraciiformes	1660
Passeres anisomyodi	1000
Passeres Oscines	4500
	9818

MAMMALIA

Monotremata	3
Marsupialia	150
Edentata	35
Rodentia	1000
Cetacea	60
Sirenia	4
Ungulata	250
Carnivora	300
Insectivora	200
Chiroptera	450
Primates	250
	2702

Supposing the fauna of the world were reduced to the 250th part of living species, then the Primates would be represented by *one* species only, and this being of course Man, his available menagerie would consist of scarcely threescore species, half of which would be Teleostean fishes. The rest would be composed of a dozen and a half of Singing-birds; half a dozen each of Lizards and Snakes; four Rodents; four non-singing neotropical passerine Birds; two species each of Wood-peckers, Humming-birds and Bats; one or two each of Parrots, Pigeons, Fowls and some other Game-birds, Kingfishers and Birds of Prey; and one species each of a Shark, Frog, Toad and Treefrog, Gecko, Ruminant and Carnivore.

Although this is a somewhat ludicrous calculation, it nevertheless indicates what may happen in time to come, it being beyond doubt that many of the smaller groups have had their day and are now on the decline, while others are on the increase and have a future before them.

INDEX

ABDIMIA, 32
Abramis, ἀβραμίς some fish in the Nile (classical), 9
Acanthidositta, 38
Acanthodi, ἀκανθώδης spiny, 6
Accipitres, rapacious birds, 33
Acentrous, without centra to the vertebrae, 5
Aceratherium, ἀ- without, κέρας horn, 47
Acipenser, ἀκκιπήσιος name of some edible fish of the Greeks, 8
Acrania, ἀ- without, κρανίον skull, 1
Acris, ἀκρίς locust, 15
Acrodont, teeth implanted upon the rim or top (ἄκρος) of the jaw, 25
Acteosaurus, ἀκταῖος dwelling on the coast, 24
Actinodon, ἀκτίς ray, spoke, 12
Actinopterygii, ἀκτίς a ray, πτερύγιον fin, 7
Adapis, a name used by Gesner, 52
Adapisoricidae, 51
Aelurus, αἴλουρος cat, 50
Aepyornis, αἰπύς high, tall, 31
Aetheospondyli, ἀήθης uncommon, σπόνδυλος vertebra, 8
Aetosaurus, ἀετός eagle (?), 19
Agama, native name, 25
Agamidae, 25
Aglossa, ἀ-γλῶσσα without tongue, 16
Aglypha, ἀ- without, γλύφω I hollow out, 28

Aistopodes, ἄιστος unseen, πόδες feet, 12
Alauda, 38
Alca, 35
Alcedo, 36
Alces, ἀλκή strength, 49
Alligator, 19
Allodon, ἄλλος different, 39
Allosaurus, ἄλλος different, 22
Allotheria, ἄλλος different, 39
Alytes, ἀλύτης a binder; in allusion to the eggs carried by the male, 15
Amblotherium, 40
Amblycephalus, ἀμβλύς stout, κεφαλή head, 29
Amblypoda, ἀμβλύς stout, πούς foot, 45
Amblypterus, ἀμβλύς stout, πτερόν fin, wing, 7
Amblyrhynchus, ἀμβλύς stout, ῥύγχος snout, bill, 25
Amblystoma, ἀμβλύς stout, στόμα mouth, 13
Ameiva, native name, 26
Amia, ἀμία name of some fish, 8
Ammodytes, ἄμμος sand, δύτης diver, 10
Amniota, ἀμνίον the membrane round the foetus, 33
Amphibia, ἀμφί both ways, βίος life, 12
Amphignathodon, ἀμφί both, γνάθος jaw, ὀδούς tooth, 15
Amphilestes, λῃστής robber, 40

Amphioxus, ἀμφί both ways or ends, ὀξύς pointed, 1
Amphirhinal, with paired nostrils, 5
Amphisbaenidae, ἀμφίς at both ends, βαίνω I walk, 27
Amphitheriidae, beasts with affinities either way, 40
Amphiuma, a native word, 14
Amphiumidae, 13
Anabas, ἀναβαίνω I climb up, 9
Anacanthini, ἀν- without, ἄκανθα spine, 9
Anallantoidea, creatures without allantois, 5
Anamnia, creatures without amnion, 5
Anaptomorphus, ἀνάπτης agitator ("stirring shape"), 52
Anarrhichas, ἀναρριχάομαι I ascend, climb (upon rocks), 9
Anas, duck, 33
Anchisaurus, ἄγχι related to, near, 22
Anchitherium, ἄγχι related, θηρίον beast, 47
Ancistrodon, ἀγκιστρώδης hook-shaped, 29
Ancylopoda, ἀγκύλος curved, πούς foot, 47
Ancylotherium, 47
Anelytropidae, ἀνέλυτρος without sheath or covering, ὤψ face (eye), 27
Anguidae, 25
Anguilla, eel (little snake), 9
Anguis, literally snake (blindworm), 26
Aniellidae, 27
Anisomyodae, ἄνισος uneven, asymmetrical, μυώδης (μῦς mussel, εἶδος likeness), 37
Anolis, native name, 25
Anomalurus, ἀνώμαλος abnormal, οὐρά tail, 43
Anomodontia, ἄνομος irregular, ὀδούς tooth, 18
Anoplotherium, ἄνοπλος unarmed, 48
Anser, goose, 33

Anthracotherium, ἄνθραξ coal, 48
Anthropoidae, ἄνθρωπος man, εἶδος shape, 53
Antiarcha, 4
Antilocapra, 49
Anura, ἄνευ without, οὐρά tail, 14
Apatornis, ἀπατάω I deceive ("misleading bird"), 31
Aphanapteryx, ἀφανής obscure, 34
Apoda, ἀ-ποδες without feet, 14
Aptenodytes, ἀ-πτήν unfledged, δύτης diver, 32
Apteryx, ἀ- without, πτέρυξ wing, 31
Aptornis, 34
Aquila, eagle, 33
Aquintocubital. The fifth cubital quill is absent, leaving a gap, 34
Aramus, 34
Archaeoceti, ἀρχαῖος old, κῆτος whale, 44
Archaeopteryx, πτέρυξ wing, 30
Archaeornithes, ἀρχαῖος old, primitive, 30
Archegosaurus, ἀρχηγός ancestor, 12
Archipterygium (Gegenbaur), the primitive, fundamental πτερύγιον little fin, 5
Arcifera, 14
Arcocentrous vertebrae, the centra of which are formed by a pair of arcualia; cf. Gastro- and Notocentrous, 7
Arctocyon, ἄρκτος bear, κύων dog, 50
Arctomys, ἄρκτος bear, μῦς mouse, 43
Arctopitheci, ἄρκτος bear, πίθηκος monkey, 53
Arctotherium, 50
Ardea, heron, 32
Argillornis, ἄργιλλος white clay, 32
Argus (in allusion to the many ocellated spots), 34
Argyropelecus, ἄργυρος silver, πέλεκυς hatchet, 9
Arthrodira, ἄρθρον joint, δειρή neck, 11

INDEX

Artiodactyla, ἄρτιος even, δάκτυλος toe, 48
Arvicola, *arvum* field, *colere* to inhabit, 43
Asio, 36
Aspidorhynchus, ἀσπίς shield, ῥύγχος snout, bill, 8
Aspredo, roughness, 9
Asterolepis, ἀστήρ star, λεπίς scale, 4
Astrapotherium, ἀστραπή lightning ("fast beast"), 45
Asymmetron, 1
Athecae, ἀ- without, θήκη shell, 21
Atlantosaurus, 22
Atractaspis, ἄτρακτος arrow, ἀσπίς the hooded, *shielded* snake, 29
Atrichia, 38
Attagis, 35
Auchenaspis, αὐχήν neck, ἀσπίς shield, 4
Auchenia, αὐχήν neck, 49
Aulacodus, αὖλαξ furrow, ὀδούς tooth, 43
Autosauri, αὐτός himself (real), 24
Aves, birds, 30

BABIRUSA, native name, 47
Balaena, whale, 44
Balaeniceps, *balaena*, φάλαινα whale, whale-headed heron, 32
Balaenoptera, πτερόν wing, fin, 44
Baptanodon, βαπτός edged, ἀνόδους toothless, 24
Barbus, barbel, 8
Basiliscus, 25
Batrachostomus, βάτραχος frog, στόμα mouth, 37
Bdellostoma, βδέλλα leech, στόμα mouth, 2
Belodon, βέλος a missile, ὀδούς, tooth, 19
Belone, βελόνη the Greek name of the garpike, 9
Belonostomus, 8
Blanus, 27
Blennius, βλέννα slime, 9
Boa, 28

Bolodon, βῶλος lump, 39
Bombinator, βόμβος a deep sound, 15
Bos, 49
Bovidae, 49
Brachylophus, βραχύς short, λόφος tuft, 25
Bradypus, βραδύς heavy, slow, 41
Branchiosaurus, βράγχιον gill, 12
Brontosaurus, βροντή thunder, astonishment, 22
Brontozoum, ζῶον animal, 22
Bubo, 36
Bucco, 37
Buceros, βοῦς ox, κερώς horned, 36
Bufo, toad, 15
Bungarus, Latinised native name, 29
Bunodonta, βουνός mound, lump (tubercular teeth), 47
Buthyrinus, 8

CACATUA, 36
Caecilia, *caecus* blind, 14
Caenolestes, καινός new, λῃστής robber, 40
Caenopithecus, καινός new, πίθηκος monkey, 52
Caenotherium, καινός new, 49
Caiman, 19
Calamoichthys, *calamus* reed, 7
Callopterus, κάλλος beauty, πτερόν fin, 8
Callorhynchus, κάλλος beauty, ῥύγχος snout, 7
Caloenas, καλός pretty, οἰνάς wild pigeon, 35
Calotes, γαλεώτης Greek name of some lizard, 25
Calyptomena, καλυπτόμενος covered, 38
Camelus, 49
Camptonotus, καμπτός flexible, 23
Cancroma, *cancroma* cancerous growth, 32
Canis, 50
Capito, *capito* a large head, 37
Capitosaurus, *capito* a large head, 13

Capra, 49
Capreolus "little goat," 49
Caprimulgus, *capra* goat, *mulgeo* I milk, 37
Capromys, κάπρος boar, μῦς, mouse, 43
Carettochelys, 21
Cariama, Latinised native name, 34
Carnivora "flesh-eaters," 49
Castor, κάστωρ beaver, 43
Castoroides "beaver-like," 43
Casuarius, 31
Catarhinae, κατά downwards, ῥίς nose, nostril, 53
Catharista, 33
Cathartes, καθαρτής scavenger, 33
Caturus, κατά downwards, οὐρά tail, 8
Cavia, Latinised native name, 43
Cavicornia, *cavus* hollow, *cornu* horn, 49
Cebochoerus, κῆβος some monkey, χοῖρος pig, 48
Cebus, κῆβος a tailed monkey, 53
Centetes, κεντητής a spiny creature, 51
Centropelma, πέλμα sole of the foot, 32
Centropus, κέντρον spur, πούς foot 36
Cephalaspis, κεφαλή head, ἀσπίς shield, 4
Cephalochorda, κεφαλή head, χορδή string, 1
Cerastes, κεράστης horned, 29
Ceratodus, κέρας horn, 11
Ceratophrys, κέρας horn, ὀφρύς eyebrow, 14
Ceratops, κέρας horn, ὤψ face, 23
Ceratopsia, 23
Ceratosaurus, κέρας horn, 22
Cercolaptes, κέρκος tail, λήπτης one who grasps, 50
Cercopithecus, κέρκος tail, πίθηκος monkey, 53
Cervicornia, *cervus* stag, *cornu* horn, 49
Cervidae, 49
Cervulus "little stag," 49

Cervus, 49
Ceryle, κηρύλος some sea-bird, 36
Cestracion, κέστρα some sea-fish, 6
Cetacea, κῆτος a sea-monster, 44
Ceyx, mythological name, 36
Chaetura, χαίτη hair, bristle, οὐρά tail, 37
Chalarodon, χαλαρός slack, loose, 25
Chalicotherium, χάλιξ gravel, 48
Chamaeleontes, χαμαι-λέων (probably little lion), 27
Chamaesaura, χαμαί low, on the ground, 25
Channa, 9
Charadrius "plover," χαράδρα a fissure on the bank, 35
Chasmorhynchus, χάσμα cleft, ῥύγχος bill, 38
Chauliodus, χαύλιος gaping, ὀδούς tooth, 9
Chauna, native name, 33
Cheirolepis, χείρ hand, λεπίς scale, 8
Chelodina, χέλυς tortoise, δίνη rotation, 21
Chelone, χελώνη turtle, 21
Chelonia, 20
Chelonidae, 21
Chelydidae, χέλυς tortoise, 21
Chelydosaurus, 12
Chelydridae, χέλυδρος a water tortoise, 20
Chimaera, 7
Chimaeropsis, ὄψις appearance, 7
Chinchilla, native name, 43
Chioglossa "χι-shaped tongue," 13
Chionis, χιών snow, 35
Chiracanthus, χείρ hand, ἄκανθα spine, 6
Chirogale, χείρ hand, γαλῆ weasel, 52
Chiroleptes, χείρ hand, λήπτης one who grasps, 14
Chiromys, 52
Chironectes, χείρ hand, νήκτης a swimmer, 40
Chiroptera, χείρ hand, πτερόν wing, 52

Chirotes, χειρωτός possessed of hands, 27
Chlamydophorus, χλαμύς mantle, φέρω I carry, 41
Chlamydosaurus, χλαμύς mantle, 25
Chlamydoselache, χλαμύς mantle, σέλαχος shark, 6
Choeropotamus, χοῖρος pig, ποταμός river, 48
Choeropus, χοῖρος pig, πούς foot, 40
Choloepus, χωλός lame, πούς foot, 41
Chondrostei, χόνδρος cartilage, ὀστέον bone, 8
Chordeiles, 37
Chordo-centra, vertebral centra formed by the calcified chorda, 5
Chrysochloris, χρυσός gold, χλωρός greenish, 51
Chrysotis, χρυσός gold, οὖς ear, 36
Ciconia, 32
Ciconiiformes, 32
Cinosternidae, κινέω I move, στέρνον breast-bone, 20
Cladodus, κλάδος branch, shoot, 5
Clamatores, clamo I shout, 38
Cleithrum, κλεῖθρον key; Gegenbaur's term for the so-called clavicle of fishes, 6
Clemmys, κλεμμύς tortoise, 20
Clepsydros, κλεψύδρα water-clock, 18
Clidastes, 24
Clupea, 9
Cnemiornis, κνημίς shinbone, 33
Cobitis, κωβίτης some kind of sardine, 9
Coccosteus, κόκκος berry, ὀστέον bone, 11
Coccystes, κοκκυστής a cuckoo-caller, 36
Coelacanthidae, κοῖλος hollow, ἄκανθα spine, 7
Coelogenys, κοῖλος hollow, γένυς cheek, 43
Coelurus, κοῖλος hollow, οὐρά tail, 22
Colius, κολιός the green woodpecker, 37

Collocalia, κολλάω I glue together, καλιά hut, nest, 37
Colossochelys, 20
Coluber, 19
Colubridae, 28
Columba, 35
Colymbus, κόλυμβος swimmer, 31
Compsognathus, κομψός elegant, γνάθος jaw, 22
Condylarthra, κόνδυλος knob of a joint, ἄρθρον joint, 45
Condylura, κόνδυλος a knob, 51
Conger, 9
Conopophaga, κώνωψ gnat, φαγεῖν to eat, 38
Conurus, κῶνος cone, οὐρά tail, 36
Coracias, κορακίας raven-like, 36
Coronella, 29
Corvus, 38
Coryphodon, κορυφή point, 45
Corythaix, 36
Cotinga, native name, 38
Cottus, κόττος thick head, 9
Coturnix, quail, 34
Craniota, κρανίον skull, 2
Crax, 34
Creodonta, κρέας flesh, ὀδούς tooth, 50
Cricetus, hamster, 43
Cricotus, κρικωτός ringed, in allusion to the vertebrae, 17
Crocidura, κροκίς tuft, οὐρά tail, 51
Crocodilia, 18
Crocodilus, 19
Crossopterygii, κροσσοι tassels, a fringe, πτερύγιον little fin, 7
Crotalus, κρόταλον rattle, 29
Crotophaga, κροτών maggot, φαγεῖν to eat, 36
Cryptobranchus, κρύπτω I hide, βράγχιον gill, 13
Cryptodira, κρύπτω I hide, δειρή neck, 20
Cryptoprocta, κρύπτω I hide, πρωκτός vent, 50
Crypturus, κρύπτω I hide, οὐρά tail, 33

Ctenacanthus, κτείς comb, ἄκανθα spine, 7
Ctenodus, κτείς comb, 11
Cuculus, 36
Cursorius, a courser, runner, 35
Cyclodus, κύκλος circle, round, 26
Cyclopterus, κύκλος circle, disk, πτερόν fin, 9
Cyclostomata, κύκλος circle, στόμα mouth, 2
Cycloturus, κύκλος circle, οὐρά tail, 41
Cygnus, 33
Cynaelurus, κύων dog, αἴλουρος cat, 50
Cynocephalus, κύων dog, κεφαλή head, 53
Cynodraco, κύων dog, 18
Cyprinus, κυπρῖνος a carp, 9
Cypselus, κύψελος a swift, κυψέλη a hollow, 37
Cystignathidae, κύστις bladder, swelling, γνάθος jaw, 14
Cystophora, κύστις bladder, φέρω I carry, 51

DACELO, 36
Dactylopterus, δάκτυλος finger, 9
Dasornis, 30
Dasypeltis, 29
Dasyprocta, πρωκτός vent, 43
Dasypus, δασύς dense, close, πούς foot, 42
Dasyurus, δασύς dense, οὐρά tail, 40
Delphinus, 44
Dendraspis, δένδρον tree, and the Aspis-snake, 29
Dendrobates "tree-walker," βαίνω I walk, 16
Dendrochelidon, χελιδών swallow, 37
Dendrocolaptes, δένδρον tree, κολάπτηρ a cutter, 28
Dendrohyrax, δένδρον tree, 75
Dendrophryniscidae, 15
Dermatemydidae, δέρμα skin (in opposition to the hard shell), 20

Dermatochelys, 21
Dermoptera, δέρμα skin, πτερόν wing, 51
Desmognathus, δεσμός a bond, joined, γνάθος jaw, 13
Diacromyodae, δι- double, ἄκρον top-end, μυώδης mussel-like. The syrinx muscles are attached to the upper and to the lower end of the bronchial semi-rings.
Diaphorapteryx, διάφορος different (from Apteryx), 34
Diatryma, τρῦμα a hole, 30
Dibamidae, δίβαμος on two legs, 27
Diceratherium, δίκερας a double horn, 47
Dichobune, δίχα bifid, βουνός lump, cusp, 48
Dicholophus, δίχα bifid, λόφος tuft, 34
Diclonius, 23
Dicotyles, δίς twice, κοτύλη a little cup (navel). In allusion to the navel and to the gland on the back, 48
Dicynodon "with two canine teeth," 18
Didelphia, δίς double, δελφύς womb, 40
Didelphys, δι- two, double, δελφύς womb, 40
Didunculus, 35
Didus, 35
Dimetrodon, 18
Dimorphodon, δι- two, μορφή shape, 23
Dinichthys, δεινός terrible, large, ἰχθύς fish, 11
Dinoceras, δεινός terrible, κέρας horn, 45
Dinomys, δεινός terrible, large, 43
Dinornithes, 31
Dinosauria, δεινός terrible, σαῦρος lizard, 22
Dinotherium, 45
Diodon "double tooth," 10
Diomedea, 32

Diplacanthus, διπλόος double, ἄκανθα spine, 6
Diplodocus, 22
Diplopterus, πτερόν wing, 7
Diplotremus, διπλόος double, τρῆμα opening, 48
Dipnoi, δίπνοος double-breathing, 11
Dipodomys, δίπους two-footed, μῦς mouse, 44
Diprotodon "two front teeth," 41
Diprotodontia, 40
Dipterus "double-fin," 11
Dipus, δίπους two-footed, 44
Discoglossus, δίσκος disk, γλῶσσα tongue, 15
Distira, 29
Distoma, δι- double, στόμα mouth, 2
Ditrema, δι- double, τρῆμα hole, 9
Dolichosauri, δολιχός long, 24
Dolichosoma, σῶμα body, 12
Dolichotis, δολιχός long, οὖς ear, 43
Dorcatherium, δορκάς a gazelle, 49
Draco, 25
Drepanis, δρεπανίς name of some bird, δρεπάνη sickle, 38
Dromaeus, δρομαῖος a runner, 39
Dromas "runner," 35
Dromatherium, δρομ- run, 40
Dryolestes, δρῦς tree, λῃστής robber, 40
Dryophis, δρῦς tree, ὄφις snake, 29
Dryopithecus, δρῦς tree, πίθηκος monkey, 54
Dyscophidae, δύσκωφος stone-deaf, 16

Echeneis, ἐχενηίς "ship holder," 9
Echidna, ἔχιδνα mythical monster, 30
Echis, 29
Edentata "toothless," 41
Elaps, 29
Elasmobranchi, ἐλασμός a plate, βράγχια gills, 5
Elephas, 45
Elginia, Elgin in Scotland, 18
Elornis, ἧλος nail, 33
Elotherium, ἧλος nail, 48
Emballonura, ἐμβάλλω I intercalate, οὐρά tail, 52
Embiotocus, ἔμβιος living, τόκος birth, 9
Emys, 20
Enaliornis, ἐν in, ἅλς sea, ὄρνις bird, 31
Engraulis, ἐγγραυλίς sardine, 9
Engystomatidae, ἐγγύς close together, 16
Enhydra, ἔνυδρις a water-snake, from ἔνυδρος living in the water, 50
Eoauchenia, ἠώς dawn, early, αὐχήν neck (Llama), 49
Eocardia, 43
Eohippos, ἠώς dawn ("early horse"), 47
Epanorthus, ἐπανορθόω I restore, 40
Epigonichthys, ἐπίγονος offspring, 1
Epomophorus, 52
Equus, 47
Erethizon, ἐρεθίζω I excite, 43
Erinaceus, 51
Eryops, εὐρύς broad, ὤψ face, 17
Erythromachus, ἐρυθρός red, -μαχος fighter, 34
Esox, pike, 9
Esthonyx, ἐσθέω I clothe, ὄνυξ claw (sheathed claw), 92
Eublepharidae, εὖ well, βλέφαρον eyelid, 25
Euchirosaurus, εὖ well, χείρ hand, σαῦρος lizard, 13
Eudyptes, εὖ well, δύπτης diver, 32
Eurycormus, εὐρύς broad, κορμός trunk, 8
Eurypyga, εὐρύς broad, πυγή tail-region, 35
Eusuchia, εὖ well, σοῦχος crocodile, 19
Eutheria, εὖ well (developed), θηρίον beast, 41
Euthynotus, εὐθύς straight, νῶτος back, 8
Exocoetus, ἐξώκοιτος "sleeping outside," 9

Falco, 33
Felis, 50
Felsinotherium, Felsino in Lombardy, 45
Feylinia, Latinised surname, 27
Ficrasfer, 10
Firmisternia, 16
Fissipedia, *fissus* split. The toes not being united by webs, 50
Fistularia, *fistula* a pipe, tube, 9
Formicarius, *formica* ant, 38
Francolinus, 34
Fratercula, 35
Fregata, 32
Fringilla, 38
Fulica, 34
Furnarius "baker," *furnus* oven, 38

Gadus, 10
Galago, native name, 52
Galbula, 37
Galeopithecus, γαλῆ weasel, πίθηκος monkey, 52
Galesaurus, γαλῆ weasel, 18
Galeus, γαλεός a shark, 6
Galliformes, 33
Gallinula, 34
Gallus, 34
Ganoidei, γάνος shine, glitter. In allusion to the enamelled scales, 7
Gastornis, 30
Gastrobranchus, γαστήρ belly, βράγχιον gill, 2
Gastrocentrous, the centra of the vertebrae are formed by a pair of ventral arcualia (interventralia), 17
Gastrosteus, γαστήρ belly, ὀστέον bone, 9
Gavialis, *gharial* (Hindustani) fish-eater, 19
Gavialosuchus, σοῦχος crocodile, 19
Gazella, 49
Geckones, 24
Gelocus, 49
Geogale, γέα earth, γαλῆ weasel, 51
Geomys, γέα earth, 44

Gerbillus, Latinised, 43
Gerrhonotus, γέρρον a shield, νῶτος back, 26
Gerrhosauridae, 26
Giraffa, 49
Glareola, *glarea* fine gravel, 35
Glauconia, γλαυκός grey, 28
Glyptodon, γλυπτός furrowed, 41
Glyptolepis, γλυπτός hollowed out, fluted, λεπίς scale, 7
Gnathostomata, γνάθος jaw, στόμα mouth, 5
Gobio, 9
Gobius, 9
Goura, 35
Gruiformes, 34
Grus, 34
Gulo, *gulo* an eater, gourmand, 50
Gymnophiona, Coecilia, γυμνός naked, ὀφίων a snake-like creature, 14
Gymnotus, γυμνός naked, 9
Gymnura, γυμνός naked, οὐρά tail, 51
Gypaëtus, γύψ vulture, ἀετός eagle, 33
Gypogeranus, γύψ vulture, γέρανος crane, 33
Gypsornis "bird from the Gypsum," 34

Hadrosaurus, ἁδρός stout, large, 22
Haematopus, αἷμα blood (red), πούς foot, 35
Halicore, ἅλς sea, κόρη maid, mermaid, 45
Halitherium, ἅλς sea, 45
Hallopus, ἅλλομαι I jump, πούς foot, 22
Hapale, ἁπαλός soft, 53
Hapaloderma, ἁπαλός soft, 37
Hapalotis, ἁπαλός soft, οὖς ear, 43
Haplodon, ἁπλόος simple, ὀδούς tooth, 43
Harpactes, ἁρπακτής robber, 37
Harpagornis, ἁρπαγή rapacity, 33
Helaletes, ἧλος nail (hoof), ἀλήτης a wanderer, 45

Heliornis, ἥλιος the sun, 35
Helladotherium, Ἑλλάς Greece, 49
Heloderma, ἧλος warty excrescence, δέρμα skin, 26
Hemiphractidae, ἡμι- half, φρακτός armed, 15
Hemipodius, ἡμίπους a half foot, 39
Heptanchus, ἑπτά seven, ἄγχω I constrict (in allusion to the gill-openings), 6
Heptatrema, ἑπτά seven, τρῆμα opening (gills), 2
Heptodon, ἑπτά seven, ὀδούς tooth, 45
Hesperornis "western bird," 31
Heterocephalus, ἕτερος different, queer, κεφαλή head, 43
Heterodactyle, ἕτερος different, abnormal, δάκτυλος toe. The first and second toes are turned back, the third and fourth standing forwards, 37
Heterostraci, ἕτερος different, ὄστρακον shell, 4
Hexanchus, ἕξ six, 6
Hipparion, ἱππάριον little horse, 47
Hippidion "a little horse," 47
Hippocampus, ἱππόκαμπος mythical sea-horse, 10
Hippopotamus, ποταμός river, 48
Hirundo, swallow, 38
Holocephali, ὅλος entire. In allusion to the palato-quadrate bar being completely fused with the cranium, 6
Holochordata, ὅλος entire, χορδή string. The chorda extending through the whole length of the animal, 1
Holoptychius, ὅλος entire, πτύχιος folded, 7
Holostei, ὅλος entire, ὀστέον bone, 8
Homacanthus, ὅμος common, joint, ἄκανθα spine, 7
Homalodontotherium, ὁμαλός even, ὀδούς tooth, 47

Homo, 54
Homoeosaurus, ὅμοιος even, equal, 18
Hoplophorus, ὅπλον weapon, φέρω I carry, 41
Hoplurus, ὅπλον weapon, οὐρά tail, 25
Hyaemoschus, 49
Hyaena, ὕαινα, 50
Hyaenarctos, ἄρκτος bear, 50
Hyaenodon "hyaena-tooth," 50
Hydraspis, ὕδωρ water, ἀσπίς shield, 21
Hydrochoerus, ὕδωρ water, χοῖρος pig, 43
Hydromedusa, 21
Hydromys "water-mouse," 43
Hydrophasianus, 35
Hydrophis, ὕδωρ water, ὄφις snake, 29
Hydropotes, ὕδωρ water, πότης a drinker, 49
Hyla, ὑλάω I bark, 15
Hylactes, ὑλάκτης one who barks, 38
Hylerpeton, ὕλη wood, forest, ἕρπω I creep, 17
Hylobates, ὕλη forest, βαίνω I walk, 53
Hylodes, ὑλώδης inhabitant of woods, 14
Hylonomus, ὑλονόμος living in the woods, 17
Hyloplesion, πλησίος near ("resembling Hyla"), 17
Hyopotamus, ὗς pig, ποταμός river, 48
Hyperoartia, ὑπερῴα the palate, ἄρτιος complete, 3
Hyperodapedon, ὑπερῴα palate, δάπεδον plane, plate, 18
Hyperotreta, ὑπερῴα the palate, τρητός perforated, 2
Hyperphalangeal, indicating the secondarily increased number of phalanges on the hands or feet beyond the normally greatest number, which amounts to five

in reptiles, three in mammals, 23, 24, 44
Hypogeomys, ὑπό below, γῆ earth, μῦς mouse, 43
Hypostomata, ὑπό below, στόμα mouth, 4
Hypselophodon, ὕψος height, λόφος projection, ὀδούς tooth, 22
Hypselornis, ὑψηλός lofty, ὄρνις bird, 31
Hypsiprymnus, ὕψι on high, πρυμνόν hindquarters, 41
Hypsirhina, ὕψι on high, ῥίς nose, 29
Hyrachius, ὕραξ a shrew, 46
Hyracodon, 46
Hyracoidea, 45
Hyracotherium, 47
Hyrax, ὕραξ a shrew (the Koni), 45
Hystricomorpha, ὕστριξ porcupine, 43

IBIDORHYNCHUS, ῥύγχος bill, 35
Ibis, 32
Ichthyes, ἰχθύς fish, 5
Ichthyodorylites, ἰχθύς fish, δόρυ lance (spike), λίθος stone, 7
Ichthyophis, ἰχθύς fish, ὄφις snake, 14
Ichthyopterygium, the typical fish-fin, 5
Ichthyornithes, 31
Ichthyosauria, 23
Ichthyosaurus, 24
Ictitherium, ἴκτις some kind of weasel, 50
Ictopsidae, ἴκτις weasel, ὄψις appearance of, 51
Iguanidae, Latinised native name, 25
Iguanodon "with teeth like Iguana," 22
Ilysia, ἰλύς mud, slime, 28
Indicator "indicator (of honey)," 37
Indris, native name, 52
Inia, native name, 44
Insectivora, 51

Intertarsal joint, 30
Irrisor, a scoffer, 36
Ischyodous, ἰσχύς strength, 7
Ischyromys, ἰσχυρός strong, 44

JACAMARHALCYON, 37

KERATERPETON, κέρας horn, ἑρπετόν creeper, snake, 12

LABRUS, λάβρος voracious, 9
Labyrinthodon, in allusion to the complicated tooth-pattern, 13
Lacertae, lizards, 25
Lacertidae, 26
Lachesis, Goddess of Fate, 29
Lagomorpha, λαγῶς hare, 42
Lagomys, λαγῶς hare, μῦς mouse, 43
Lagostomus, στόμα mouth, 43
Laosaurus, λάω I look at, 22
Lariosaurus, 23
Larus, gull, 35
Lemuravus, avus ancestor, 52
Lemures, lemur a nocturnal spectre, 52
Lepidosiren, λεπίς scale, 11
Lepidosteus, λεπίς scale, ὀστέον bone, 8
Lepidotus, λεπιδωτός scaly, 8
Lepospondyli (Stegocephali), 12, (Prosauria) 17, λέπος a husk, rind, σπόνδυλος vertebra
Lepospondylous "thin-shelled," 12
Leptocardia, λεπτός thin, καρδία heart, 1
Leptodon, λεπτός thin, 47
Leptomeryx, μηρός thigh, shank, 49
Leptoptilus, λεπτός thin, πτίλον feather, 32
Leptosoma, λεπτός thin, σῶμα body, 36
Lepus, hare, 43
Lestris, λῃστρίς piratical, 35
Leuciscus, λευκός white ("whitefish"), 9
Lialis, 27
Limicolae "mud-inhabitants," 35
Limosa, limus mud, 35

Liodon, λεῖος smooth, ὀδούς tooth, 24
Liopelma, λεῖος smooth, πέλμα the sole of the foot, 15
Lissamphibia, λισσός smooth, naked, 13
Lissencephalous, λισσός smooth (without furrows), ἐγκέφαλος brain, 42
Lithornis, λίθος stone ("fossil bird"), 33
Litopterna, λιτός smooth, plain, πτέρνα heel, 46
Lophiodon, λόφιον small hill, lump, 46
Lophius, λοφιά the mane on the neck, 9
Lophobranchii, λόφος bunch, βράγχια gills, 10
Lophopsittacus, λόφος tuft, ψιττακός parrot, 36
Loris, native name, 52
Lorius, 36
Lota, loach, 10
Lutra, otter, 50
Lycaon, λύκος wolf, 50
Lycosaurus, λύκος wolf, 18

Macacus, native name, 53
Machaerodus, μάχαιρα a curved sword, 50
Macrauchenia, μακρός long, αὐχήν neck, 46
Macroclemmys, μακρός long, κλεμμύς tortoise, 20
Macropoma, μακρός long, πῶμα cover, lid, 7
Macropristis, πρίστις saw, 41
Macropus, μακρός large, πούς foot, 41
Macroscelides, μακρός long, σκέλος shank, 51
Macrotherium, 48
Malapterurus, μαλός soft, πτερόν fin, οὐρά tail, 9
Mammalia, mamma breast, teat, 39
Manatus, 45
Manis, a spectre, 41
Mantella, 16

Marsipobranchii, μάρσιπος pouch, basket, βράγχια gills, 2
Marsupialia, marsupium pouch, 40
Mastodon, μαστός nipple, ὀδούς tooth, 46
Mastodonsaurus, 13
Megacephalon, κεφαλή head, 34
Megalaema, μέγας large, 37
Megalichthys, μέγας large, 7
Megalosaurus, μέγας large, 22
Megalurus, μέγας large, οὐρά tail, 8
Megapodius, μέγας large, πούς foot, 34
Megatherium, μέγας large, 41
Meleagris, mythological name, 34
Meles, badger, 50
Meliphaga, μέλι honey, φαγεῖν to eat, 38
Mellivora, mel honey, vorare to swallow, 50
Meniscotherium, μηνίσκος a little moon, 46
Menobranchus, μένω I remain, βράγχιον gill, 14
Menopoma, μένω I remain, πῶμα cover, lid, 14
Menura, μήνη moon, οὐρά tail, 38
Mephitis "noxious smell," 50
Merops, bee-eater, 36
Merycopotamus, μήρυξ a ruminating fish, ποταμός river, 48
Mesembriornis, μεσημβρία noon, 31
Mesites, μεσίτης mediator. In allusion to the uncertain taxonomic position, 34
Mesohippos, μέσος middle, 47
Mesonyx, μέσος middle, ὄνυξ claw, 50
Mesopithecus, 53
Mesoplodon, μέσος middle, ὅπλον weapon, 44
Mesosauri, 23
Metatheria "after, later, beasts," 40
Metriorhynchus, μέτριος moderate, ῥύγχος bill, 19
Miacis, 50
Microchoerus, μικρός small, χοῖρος pig, 52

Microlestes, μικρός small, λῃστής robber, 39
Microsauri, 12
Mixipterygium, Gegenbaur's term for the copulatory claspers of Elasmobranchi, μίξις copulation, 5
Mixosaurus "mixed, intermediate, Saurian," 24
Moloch, 25
Molossus, 52
Molva, Latinised from French *morue*, Italian *molua*, hence the mediaeval *morrhua*, 9
Momotus, native name, 36
Monodelphia, μόνος single, unpaired, δελφύς womb, 41
Monodon, μόνος single, ὀδούς tooth, 44
Monorhina, μόνος single, unpaired, ῥίς nostril, 2
Monotremata, μόνος single, unpaired, τρῆμα opening (cloacal), 39
Mormyrus, μορμύρος some sea-fish, μορμύρω I murmur, 9
Moropus, μωρός sluggish, πούς foot, 41
Morosaurus, μωρός stupid, 22
Morotherium, μωρός stupid, 41
Mosasauri, *Mosa* the river Maas, 24
Moschus, 49
Mullus, 9
Muraena, 9
Mus, 43
Muscardinus, 43
Muscicapa, *musca* fly, *capere* to catch, 38
Musophaga, *musa* the banana, φαγεῖν to eat, 36
Mustela, weasel, 50
Mustelus, weasel, 6
Mycetes, μυκητής a roarer, 53
Myliobates, μυλίας millstone, βατίς a ray, 6
Mylodon, μύλος millstone, 41
Myobatrachus, μῦς mouse, βάτραχος frog, 15
Myogale, μῦς mouse, γαλῆ weasel, 51

Myomorpha "mouse-shaped animals," 43
Myopotamus, μῦς mouse, ποταμός river, 43
Myoxus, dormouse, 43
Myriacanthus, μυρίος countless, ἄκανθα spine, 7
Myrmecobius, μύρμηξ ant, βιόω I live (on), 40
Myrmecophaga, μύρμηξ ant, φαγεῖν to eat, 41
Mystacoceti, μύσταξ moustache, κῆτος whale, 44
Myxine, μυξῖνος a slimy fish, μύξα slime, 2
Myxinoides, 2

Naja, *nag* (Hindustani) snake, 29
Necrogymnurus, νεκρός dead, γυμνός naked, οὐρά tail, 51
Necrolemur, νεκρός corpse, 52
Necturus, νήχω I swim, οὐρά tail, 14
Neornithes "modern birds," 30
Nerophis, νηρός wet, ὄφις snake, 10
Nesodon, νῆσος island, 45
Nesomys, νῆσος island, μῦς mouse, 43
Nestor, 36
Nimravus, 51
Nomarthra, νόμος custom, ἄρθρον joint, 41
Nothosauri, νόθος spurious, 23
Notocentrous, the vertebral centrum is formed by dorsal arcualia (interdorsalia) only, 12
Notopteris, νῶτον back, πτερόν wing, 52
Notornis, νότος south, 34
Notoryctes, νότον south, ὀρυκτήρ a digger, 40
Nototherium, νότος south, 41
Nototrema, νῶτον back, τρῆμα hole, 15
Numenius, 35
Numida, 34
Nycteris, νυκτερίς a nocturnal animal, 52
Nyctibius, νύξ night, βιόω I live, 37

Nycticebus, νύξ night, κῆβος monkey, 52
Nyctiornis, νύξ night, ὄρνις bird, 36
Nyctipithecus, νύξ night, πίθηκος monkey, 53

OCEANITES, 32
Octodon, ὀκτώ eight, ὀδούς tooth, 43
Ocydromus, ὠκύς fast, δρόμος a runner, 34
Odontoceti "toothed whales," 44
Odontolcae, ὀδούς tooth, ὁλκός furrow. The teeth standing in furrows, not in separate alveoli, 31
Odontopteryx, ὀδούς tooth, πτέρυξ wing, 32
Oedicnemus, οἶδος swelling, κνήμη shank, 25
Onchus, ὄγκος barb, 7
Ophiderpeton, ὄφις snake, ἑρπετόν creeper, snake, 12
Ophidia, 28
Ophiocephalus, ὄφις snake, κεφαλή head, 9
Ophisaurus, 26
Ophthalmosaurus, ὀφθαλμός eye, 24
Opisthocoelous, vertebrae hollow at the hind end, 15
Opisthocomus, ὄπισθεν behind, κόμη hair, 34
Opisthoglypha, ὄπισθεν behind, γλύφη a furrow (in the hinder teeth), 28
Orca, 44
Oreodon, ὄρος mountain (lump), ὀδούς tooth, 48
Oreopithecus, ὄρος mountain, 53
Ornithichnites, ἴχνος track, spoor, 22
Ornithocheirus, χείρ hand, 23
Ornithodelphia, ὄρνις bird, δελφύς womb, 39
Ornithomimus "mimicking a bird," 23
Ornithopoda "bird - footed creatures," 22
Ornithopsis, ὄψις appearance of, 22
Ornithorhynchus, 39

Ornithosuchus, σοῦχος crocodile, 19
Ortalida, 34
Orthagoriscus, ὀρθαγορίσκος a little pig, 10
Orthopoda, ὀρθός upright, πούς foot, 22
Ortyx, ὄρτυξ quail, 34
Orycteropus, ὀρυκτήρ a digger, 41
Oryzorictes, ὄρυζα rice, ὀρύκτης a digger, 51
Oscines "singing birds," 38
Osmerus, ὀσμηρός smelling, smelt, 9
Osteolaemus, ὀστέον bone, λαιμός throat, 19
Osteolepis, ὀστέον bone, λεπίς scale, 7
Osteorhachis, ῥάχις spine (vertebra), 8
Osteostraci, ὀστέον bone, ὄστρακον shell, 4
Ostracion, ὀστράκιον a little shell, 10
Ostracodermi, ὄστρακον shell, δέρμα skin, 4
Otaria, ὠτάριον a little ear, 51
Otis, bustard, 35
Otocyon, οὖς ear, κύων dog, 50
Otus, ὠτός eared owl, οὖς ear, 36
Oudenodon, οὐδέν nothing (absent), ὀδούς tooth, 18
Ovibos "sheep-ox," musk-ox, 49
Ovis, sheep, 49
Oxyclaenus, ὀξύς sharp, pointed, 50

PACHYRUCOS, παχύς thick, 42
Palaeudyptes, εὖ well, δύπτης diver, 32
Palaelodus, 33
Palaeohatteria "ancient Hatteria," παλαιός old, *Hatter* a surname, 17
Palaeolagus, λαγῶς a hare, 43
Palaeonictis, ἴκτις some kind of weasel, 50
Palaeoniscus, ὀνίσκος some sea-fish, 8
Palaeophis, παλαιός old, ὄφις snake, 28
Palaeospheniscus, σφηνίσκος small wedge, 32

Palaeospondylus, παλαιός old, σπόνδυλος vertebra, 3
Palaeosyops, ὖς pig, ὤψ appearance of, 47
Palaeotherium, παλαιός old, ancient, 47
Palamedea, Παλαμήδης name of a classical hero, 33
Pandion, Πανδίων an Athenian king's name, 33
Parasuchia, παρά aside of, σοῦχος crocodile, 19
Pareiosauri, παρειά cheek, 18
Parra, classical name of some bird, 35
Patagona, from Patagonia, 37
Pavo, peacock, 34
Pecora, *pecus* cattle, 49
Pedetes, πηδητής a jumper, 44
Pedionomus "dwelling in plains," from πεδίον and νέμομαι, 34
Pelagornis, πέλαγος sea, ὄρνις bird, 32
Pelecanidae, 32
Pelobates, πηλός mud, βαίνω I walk, 15
Pelodytes, πηλός mud, δύτης a diver, 15
Pelomedusidae, πηλός mud, 21
Pelycodus, πέλυξ axe, hatchet, ὀδούς tooth, 53
Pelycosauri, πέλυξ axe, hatchet. In allusion to the prominent canine teeth, 18
Penelope, 34
Perameles, πήρα bag, *meles* badger, 40
Perca, perch, 9
Perciformes, 9
Perdix, partridge, 34
Periophthalmus, ὀφθαλμός eye, 9
Periptychus, πτύξ fold, 46
Perissodactyla, περισσός uneven, odd (toed), 46
Perodicticus, πηρός maimed, mutilate, δεικτικός ostensive (index finger), 53
Petaurus, πέταυρον perch, springboard, 40

Petromyzontes, πέτρος stone, μύζω I suck, 3
Pezophaps, πεζο-φάψ "foot-pigeon," 36
Phacochoerus, φακός a wart, χοῖρος pig, 48
Phaeton, Φαέθων the shiny one (mythological), 32
Phalacrocorax, φαλακρός bald-headed, κόραξ raven, 32
Phalangista, in allusion to the elongated phalanges, 40
Phalaropus, φαλαρός shiny, πούς foot, 35
Phaneroglossa, φανερός visible, γλῶσσα tongue, 14
Phaneropleuron, φανερός obvious, πλευρόν side, 11
Pharomacrus, φάρος lighthouse, μακρός long. In allusion to the shiny plumage, 37
Pharyngognathi, φάρυγξ gullet, throat, γνάθος jaw, 9
Phascolarctos, φάσκωλος bag, ἄρκτος bear, 40
Phascolomys, φάσκωλος bag, μῦς mouse, 41
Phascolotherium, φάσκωλος bag, 40
Phasianus, 34
Phenacodus, φέναξ impostor, humbug, 46
Philepitta, 38
Phoca, seal, 51
Phocaena, φώκαινα porpoise, 44
Phoenicophaes, φοινικοφαής purple-shining, 36
Phoenicopterus, flamingo, φοῖνιξ red, πτερόν wing, 33
Pholidosaurus, φολίς scaly covering, 19
Phororhacos, φέρω I carry, 24
Phractamphibia, φρακτός armoured, 12
Phrynosoma, φρύνη toad, σῶμα body, 25
Phyllopteryx, φύλλον leaf, πτέρυξ fin, 10

Phyllostoma, φύλλον leaf, στόμα mouth, 52
Physeter, φυσητήρ a blower, 44
Physoclysti, φῦσα an air-passage, bellows, κλύω I hear, 9
Physostomi, φῦσα an air-passage, στόμα mouth (communicating with the air-bladder), 8
Picumnus, mythological name, 37
Picus, woodpecker, 37
Pinnipedia, *pinna* fin, 51
Pipa, native name, 16
Pipra, 38
Pisces, 5
Pithecanthropus, πίθηκος monkey, ἄνθρωπος man, 54
Pitta, 38
Placentalia, 41
Placodontia, 18
Placodus, πλάξ plate, ὀδούς tooth, 18
Plagiaulax, πλάγιος oblique, αὖλαξ furrow, 39
Plagiostomi, πλάγιος transverse, 5
Platalea "spoonbill," 32
Platanista, πλατανιστής the dolphin of the Ganges, 44
Platecarpus, πλάτη blade, καρπός wrist, 24
Platycercus, πλατύς broad, κέρκος tail, 36
Platyrhinae, πλατύς broad, ῥίς nose, nostril, 53
Platysomus, πλατύς flat, broad, σῶμα body, 8
Platysternidae, πλατύς broad, στέρνον breastbone, 20
Plecotus, πλέκω I connect, οὖς ear, 52
Plectognathi, πλεκτός connected, fixed, γνάθος jaw, 10
Plesindapis, πλησίος akin to (Adapis), 53
Plesiochelys, πλησίος akin to, χέλυς tortoise, 21
Plesiosauria, πλησίος approaching, akin to, 23

Plethodon, πλῆθος plenty, 13
Pleuracanthus, πλευρόν side, ἄκανθα spine, 5
Pleurodira, πλευρόν side, δειρή neck, 21
Pleurodont. The teeth are implanted against the inner side of the jaw, 26
Pleuronectes, πλευρόν side, νήκτης a swimmer, 10
Pliohippos "Pliocene horse," 47
Pliopithecus "Pliocene monkey," 54
Plioplatecarpus, 24
Pliosaurus, 23
Plotus, πλωτός swimming, 32
Podargus, πόδαργος swift-footed, 37
Podicipes, *podex* buttock, *pes* foot, 32
Poebrotherium, πόα herb, 49
Pogonorhynchus, πώγων beard, ῥύγχος bill, 37
Polychrus, πολύχροος many-coloured, 25
Polymastodon, πολύς many, μαστός teat, nipple, 39
Polyodon, πολύς many, ὀδούς tooth, 8
Polyprotodontia, πολύς many, πρῶτος first, ὀδούς tooth (numerous incisors), 40
Polypterus, πολύς many, πτερόν fin (dorsal fins), 7
Polyptychodon, πτύξ a fold, 23
Polytrema, πολύς many, τρῆμα hole, 2
Pontoporia, ποντοπόρος passing over the sea, πόντος sea, πορεύω I ferry across, 44
Postacetabular, the primary iliosacral connexion lies behind, tailwards from the acetabulum, in reptiles and birds (Gegenbaur), 17
Postcentra, the central vertebral disks which carry no arches, 8
Potamogale, ποταμός river, γαλῆ weasel, 51
Preacetabular, the primary ilio-

sacral connexion lies in front of, headwards from, the acetabulum (Gegenbaur), 14, 39
Precentra, the vertebral central disks which carry the dorsal and ventral arches, 8
Priodon, πρίων a saw, 42
Pristis, πρίστις a saw, 6
Proaelurus, αἴλουρος cat, 51
Proboscidea, προβοσκίς nose, elongated snout, 45
Procamelus, 49
Procellariae, *procella* storm, 32
Procoelous, κοῖλος hollow; hollow in front, 15
Procyon, κύων dog, 50
Proechidna, 39
Proganochelys, γάνος shine, glitter, 21
Proherodius, 32
Propelargus, πελαργός stork, 32
Propithecus, 53
Prorastomus, πρῷρα prow, bow, στόμα mouth, 45
Proreptilia "early, incipient reptiles," 17
Prosauri "early lizards," 17
Proselachii, 5
Protapirus, 46
Proteles, προτελής an animal for sacrifice, 50
Proteroglypha, πρότερος foremost, γλυφή furrow, 29
Proterotherium, 46
Proteus, mythological, 14
Protodonta, 40
Protohippos "early horse," 47
Protopterus, πρῶτος earliest, πτερόν fin, 11
Protoreodon, 48
Protorosaurus, πρῶτος first, ὥρα spring (dawn), 17
Protosphargis, 21
Protospondyli, πρῶτος earliest, σπόνδυλος vertebra, 8
Protostega, στέγη roof, covering, 21
Prototheria, πρῶτος first, early, θηρία beasts, 38

Protypotherium, 42
Proviverra, 50
Psammophis, ψάμμος sand, ὄφις snake, 29
Psarisomus, ψάρ some starling, σῶμα body, 38
Psephoderma, ψῆφος pebble, δέρμα skin, 21
Psephophorus, ψῆφος a pebble (granulation), 21
Pseudaelurus, αἴλουρος cat, 51
Pseudis, ψευδής false, 14
Pseudobranchus, ψεῦδος deceit, βράγχιον gill, 14
Pseudocentrous, vertebrae without real centra, 12
Pseudophryne, φρύνη toad, 15
Pseudopus, ψεῦδος deceit, πούς foot, 26
Pseudosuchia, σοῦχος crocodile, 19
Psittaci, ψιττακός parrot, 36
Psophia, ψόφος sound, noise, 34
Pteranodon, πτερόν wing, ἀν-όδους toothless, 23
Pteraspis, πτερόν wing, ἀσπίς shield, 4
Pterichthys, πτερόν wing, ἰχθύς fish, 4
Pterocles, πτερόν wing, κλείς key, bolt, 35
Pterodactyli, πτερόν wing, δάκτυλος finger, 23
Pteromys, πτερόν wing, μῦς mouse, 43
Pteroptochus, πτωκάς timorous, 38
Pteropus, πτερόν wing, πούς foot, 52
Pterosauria, πτερόν wing, 23
Ptilocercus, πτίλον tuft or down, κέρκος tail, 51
Ptyctodus, πτυκτός folded, 6
Pycnodus, πυκνός dense, 8
Pygopus, πυγή hindquarters, πούς foot, 27
Python, mythological name, 28
Pythonomorpha, 24

QUINTOCUBITAL. The cubital quills form an unbroken series. *See* Aquintocubital, 34

INDEX

RAIAE, rays, 6
Rallus, 34
Rana, 16
Rangifer, French *ranche* rack, ladder, Lat. *fero* I bear, 9
Ranidens "frog-tooth," 13
Ratitae, *rates* a raft, flat-bottomed, keelless vessel, 30
Regalecus, Lat. *rex* king, and Latinised *halec* a herring (in allusion to the popular name "king of the herrings"), 49
Reptilia, *repere* to creep, 17
Rhachiodon, 29
Rhacophorus, ῥάκος a rag, lappet, 16
Rhamphastus, ῥάμφος a curved beak, 37
Rhamphorhynchus, ῥάμφος strong bill, ῥύγχος snout, bill, 23
Rhea, mythological name, 30
Rhinoceros, ῥίς nose, κέρας horn, 47
Rhinochetus, ῥίς nose, ὀχετός a tube, 35
Rhinoderma, ῥίς nose, δέρμα skin, 16
Rhinolophus, ῥίς nose, λόφος tuft, 52
Rhinophis, ῥίς nose, ὄφις snake, 28
Rhizomys, ῥίζα root, 43
Rhodeus, ῥόδεος rose-coloured, 9
Rhombus, 10
Rhynchaea, 35
Rhynchocephali, ῥύγχος strong snout, κεφαλή head, 18
Rhynchops, contracted from ῥύγχος bill, ψάλις scissors, 35
Rhynchosaurus, 18
Rhynchotus, ῥύγχος bill, 33
Rhytina, ῥυτίς a wrinkle, fold. In allusion to the bark-like skin, 45
Rhytiodus, ῥυτίς wrinkle, 45
Ribodon, 46
Rodentia, *rodere* to gnaw, 42
Ruminantia, *ruminare* to chew, 48
Rupicapra, 49
Rupicola, *rupes* rock, *colere* to inhabit, 38

SALAMANDRA, 13
Salamandrella, 13
Salmo, salmon, 9
Samotherium, the island of Samos, 49
Sauria, σαῦρος lizard, 24
Sauropoda, 22
Scarus, wrass, 9
Scelidosaurus, σκελίς rib, 22
Scelidotherium, σκελίς rib, 41
Scincidae, σκίγκος some lizard, 26
Sciuroides, 43
Sciuromorpha, 43
Sciurus, squirrel, 43
Scolopax, σκολόπαξ the woodcock, σκόλοψ a pole (the long bill), 35
Scomber, mackerel, 9
Scombresox, *scomber* mackerel, *esox* pike, 9
Scopelus, σκόπελος a rock in the sea, 9
Scopus, σκοπός inspector, sentinel, 32
Scyllium, σκύλιον some shark or dogfish, 6
Sebastes, σεβαστός august, 9
Selachii, τὰ σελάχη the sharks, 5
Selenidera, σελήνη moon, δειρή neck, 37
Selenodonta, σελήνη moon, 48
Semnopithecus, σεμνός sacred, πίθηκος monkey, 53
Sepedon, σηπεδών putrefaction, 29
Serranus, *serra* a saw, 9
Siluridae, σίλουρος the sheat fish, 9
Simaedosaurus, 17
Simia, monkey, 54
Simiae, 53
Siren, 14
Sirenia, 44
Sirenoidei, 11
Sivatherium "Shiva's beast," 49
Smilerpeton, σμίλη knife, 17
Smilodon, 51
Solea, sole, 10
Solenodon, σωλήν tube, runnel, 51

Sorex, shrew, 51
Spalax, σπάλαξ a mole, 43
Spelerpes, σπήλαιον cave, ἕρπω I crawl, 13
Sphargis, a fancy name, 21
Spheniscus, σφηνίσκος diminutive of σφήν sickle, wedge (-shaped bill), 32
Sphenodon, σφήν wedge, 18
Sphenosaurus, σφήν wedge, sickle, 12
Squalodon, *squalus* shark, *squalere* to be rough, ὀδούς tooth, 44
Squaloraia, *squalus* shark, 7
Squatina, Pliny's name, 6
Steatornis, στέαρ fat, 36
Steganopodes, στεγανός closely covered, sheathed. In allusion to all the four toes being webbed together, 32
Stegocephali, στέγος roof, κεφαλή head. The cranium being roofed over by dermal bones, 12
Stegosauri, στέγος, 22
Steneosaurus, στένος a narrow place, 19
Stereospondyli (Prosauria), στερεός solid, σπόνδυλος vertebra, 17
Stereospondyli (Stegocephali), 13
Sterna, tern, 35
Stringops, στρίξ an owl, ὤψ face, 36
Strix, 36
Struthio, ostrich, 31
Stylinodon, στῦλος pillar, ἴς (genitive ἰνός) fibre, 42
Subclamatores "lower than the typical Clamatores," 37
Suboscines "lower than the typical Oscines," 38
Sula, gannet, 32
Sus, 48
Syngnathus "fused jaw," 10
Synodontis, σύν with, together. Teeth fused together, 9
Syrrhaptes, συρράπτω I sew together (in allusion to the toes), 35

TACHYPETES, ταχύς quick, πέτομαι I fly, 32
Talegallus, 34
Talpa, the mole, 51
Tamias, ταμίας caretaker, 43
Tapirus, 46
Tarsius. In allusion to the much elongated tarsus, 53
Tatusia, native name, 42
Tectobranchi, *tectus* covered. The gills being covered by an operculum, 6
Teleosaurus, τέλεος complete, 19
Teleostei, τέλεος complete, ὀστέον bone, 8
Teleostomi, τέλεος terminal, with reference to the position of the mouth, in opposition to Plagiostomi, 7
Telerpeton, τέλος end, ἑρπετόν creeper, 17
Temnospondyli, τέμνω I cut, separate, σπόνδυλος vertebra, 12
Tejidae, native name, 26
Teratoscincus, τέρας a marvel, 25
Testudinidae, 20
Tetraceros, τετρα- four, κέρας horn, 49
Tetrao, 34
Tetrapoda, Credner's name for "four-footed creatures," in opposition to the fishes which have fins, 12
Tetrodon "four-tooth," 10
Thalassochelys, θάλασσα sea, χέλυς tortoise, 21
Thecophora, θήκη chest, case, φέρω I carry, 20
Theriodomys, θηριώδης beast-like, 43
Theriodontia, θηρίον a beast, 18
Theromorpha, θήρ a beast, μορφή shape, 18
Theropoda, θήρ a mammal, πούς foot, 23
Thinocorys, θίς shore, κόρυς helmet, 35

Thylacinus, θύλακος bag, 40
Thylacoleo " the bag- (marsupial) lion," 41
Thynnus, θύννος the tunny, 9
Thyroptera, θύρα door, valve, 52
Tiga, 37
Tiliqua, 26
Tillodontia, τίλλω I pluck out, tear off, 42
Tillotherium, 42
Tinamus, native name, 33
Tinca, tench, 9
Titanichthys "gigantic fish," 11
Titanotherium, 46
Todus, native name, 36
Tomistoma, τομίς knife-edge, στόμα mouth, 19
Torpedo, 6
Toxodon, τόξον a bow, 45
Toxotes, τοξότης bowman, shooter, 9
Trachinus, τραχύς rough, spiky, 9
Trachysaurus, τραχύς rough, 26
Tragulidae, 48
Tragulus, τράγος a he-goat, 49
Trematosaurus, τρῆμα a hole, 13
Treron, τρήρων shy, 35
Triceratops, τρι- three, κέρας horn, ὤψ face, 23
Trichechus, τρίχες plural of θρίξ hair, ἔχω I have. In allusion to the bristly mouth, 51
Trichoglossus, θρίξ hair, γλῶσσα tongue, 36
Triconodon "three-coned tooth," 40
Triconodonta, 40
Triisodon, τρι- three, ἴσος equal, 50
Trimerorhachis, ῥάχις the spine (" three-pieced vertebra"), 13
Tringa, 35
Trionychoidea, 21
Trionyx, τρι-όνυξ three-clawed, 21
Triton, 13
Trituberculata, 40
Tritylodon, τύλη lump (tooth with three cusps), 39
Trochilus, classical name, 37

Troglodytes, τρωγλοδύτης a cave-dweller, 54
Trogon, τρώγων gnawing, 37
Trogonophis, 27
Trogontia, τρώγων gnawing, 42
Tropidonotus, τρόπις keel, νῶτος back, 29
Trygon, τρυγών the spiny ray, 6
Tupaja, 51
Turdus, 38
Turnices, 34
Typhlops, τυφλός blind, ὤψ eye, 28
Typhlosaurus, τυφλός blind, 27
Typotherium, τύπος pattern, type, 42
Tyrannus, 38

UINTATHERIUM, Uintah mountains in Utah, 45
Undina, 7
Ungulata, *unguis* claw, hoof, 45
Upupa, 36
Urocordylus, κορδύλος some kind of lizard (hence κροκόδειλος), 12
Urodela, οὐρά tail, δῆλος visible, plain, 13
Uromastix, οὐρά tail, μάστιξ whip, 25
Uropeltis, οὐρά tail, πέλτη a small shield, 28
Uroplatidae, πλατύς flat, 25
Ursus, bear, 50

VAMPYRUS, 52
Vanellus, 35
Varanus, *ouaran* (Arabic) = lizard, 26
Vespertilio, bat, from *vesper*, ἕσπερος evening, 52
Vesperugo, bat, 52
Viperidae, 29
Viverra, 50
Vulturidae, 33

XANTHUSIA, Xanthus a surname, 26

Xenacanthus, ξένος strange, ἄκανθα spine, spike, 5
Xenarthra, ξένος strange, abnormal, ἄρθρον joint, 41
Xenicus, ξενικός outlandish, 38
Xenopus, ξένος strange, πούς foot, 16
Xenosaurus, ξένος strange, 25
Xiphias, ξιφίας the swordfish, 9
Xiphodon, ξίφος sword, 48

Yunx, ἴυγξ the wryneck, 37

Zamenis, 29
Zanclodon, 22
Zeuglodon, ζεύγλη the strap, loop of the yoke, 44
Zeus, 9
Ziphius, ξιφιός the swordfish, 44
Zoarces, ζωαρκής life-preserving, 22
Zonosaurus, ζώνη girdle, 26
Zonurus, ζώνη girdle, οὐρά tail, 26
Zygaena, ζύγαινα the hammer-headed shark, 6

THE END

www.ingramcontent.com/pod-product-compliance
Lightning Source LLC
Chambersburg PA
CBHW030254170426
43202CB00009B/734